NLP – Neuro-Linguistic Programming

~

Mastering the NLP by learning Body Language, Persuasion and Manipulation with Mind Control.

Maximize your potential and discover the secrets of Emotional Influence.

Ted Goleman

Table of contents

Introduction

Dark Psychology studies the predatory, exploitative, and sometimes criminal behavior and psyche of people who victimize others. Every human can potentially mistreat other humans and, more generally, living things. While many of us can control or sublimate this impulse, others cannot resist, acting on it instead.

Dark Psychology tries to comprehend the thoughts, emotions, and observations that lead to predatory conduct that contradicts contemporary understandings of human behavior. Dark Psychology presupposes that criminal, abusive, and deviant behaviors are premeditated, astute, and persistent 99.99% of the time. However, the remaining 0.01%, Dark Psychology proposes, submits to atrocious acts without reason or intent. This hypothesis has been coined the Dark Singularity.

Dark Psychology proposes that every person has a repository of malevolent aim towards others ranging from slightly intrusive and passing ruminations to unadulterated and psychopathic actions that lack reason. This is known as the Dark Continuum. Moderating components acting as accelerants or attractants to moving toward the Dark Singularity, and where an individual's behaviors fall on the Dark Continuum, is the Dark Factor.

Dark Psychology envelops everything that makes us who we are with regards to our dark side. All societies, religions, and all humankind have this disease. From birth to death, we all have a hidden insidious, and sometimes criminal or neurotic, side. In contrast to religious principles and contemporary sociological theories, Dark Psychology presents a third philosophical development that sees these practices differently.

Dark Psychology states that there are individuals who behave in this way but not for power, money, sex, revenge, or another known reason. They behave in this way without an objective. In other words, their ends don't justify their means. There are individuals who disregard and harm others just for the sake of it. The potential to hurt others without cause, explanation, or reason is inside each of us. Dark Psychology presumes this dark potential is unbelievably complicated and much harder to characterize.

Dark Psychology assumes that we all have the potential for predator behaviors and this potential knows our thoughts, feelings, and judgments. As you will soon read, we all have this potential, yet just a few of us follow through on them. We all have had ruthless impulses. We all have considered seriously hurting others. If you are honest with yourself, you will acknowledge that you have had these intolerable impulses.

That fact notwithstanding, we tend to view ourselves as a generous species; therefore, one might not want to accept that the desire to manipulate exists. Nevertheless, we all have these inclinations but fortunately never follow through on them. According to Dark

Psychology, there are individuals who have these same thoughts, emotions, and discernments, yet follow through on them in either deliberate or rash ways. This is what separates them from others.

Dark Psychology sets that this predator style is purposive and has some levelheaded, objective arranged inspiration. Religion, philosophy, and neuropsychology have tried to define Dark Psychology. Most human behavior, both good and evil, is intentional and goal-oriented; however, Dark Psychology hypothesizes that there is a zone where purposive and goal-oriented actions become ill-defined. There is a continuum of Dark Psychology exploitation ranging from merely passing thoughts to genuine psychopathic abnormality with no evident reason or motive. The Dark Continuum conceptualizes the philosophy of Dark Psychology.

Dark Psychologists acknowledge that submission to evil is unpredictable in both the predators' identities, as well as how far they will go with no sense of morality to hold them back. Some people irrationally assault, murder, torment, and abuse. Dark Psychology views these people as predators hunting for human prey. Humans are especially dangerous to themselves and other living things. Dark Psychology aims to address the many reasons behind this.

Chapter 1

Overview Of The History And Origins Of NLP

History of Neuro-linguistic Programming

This is probably because of various life challenges that people have to go through back then. There was a growing number of people with Depression, Schizophrenia, Bipolar Disorders, and other personality disorders who need psychotherapy. However, this growing demand was a problem to psychotherapists back then since there was not enough of them to handle every case. There was still a lack of awareness about mental health, especially in remote places. People were still skeptic about getting help from psychotherapists even when they extremely need it. Hence, the conditions of people got worse in some areas, alarming psychotherapists to provide immediate help. There were no specific guidelines or training yet to people who wanted to help mentally challenged individuals. This pushed the need to create a model to help aspiring psychotherapists to be efficient in their line of work to help those in need from their localities.

Actually, Abraham Maslow already had this idea in 1943 when he studied and proposed his theory on the Hierarchy of Needs. He modeled about

60 "Self-realized" people who can help in the Humanistic Psychology movement by raising awareness about the positive approach of psychoanalysis and behaviorism. Maslow aimed to break the pessimistic view in dealing with mental disorders. Hence, pushing the third force in psychology way back in 1961.

The two proponents of NLP started to identify communication patterns, attitude and all the thinking characteristics of Satir, Erickson, and Perls. Finally, they were able to extract a set of skills, techniques, and beliefs they could use to further their studies. Bandler and Grinder named these as Neuro-linguistic Programming.

Four Waves of Neuro-linguistic Programming

Over the years of its improvement, Bandler and Grindler organized its foundation into four waves:

The first wave created was NLPure which started in 1972. Its main topic is about "Success and Enthusiasm." To raise awareness about the importance of NLP, Anthony Robins conducted and developed several motivational seminars all over the world with very large crowds.

The third wave in the Neuro-linguistic Programming movement is known as the NLPeace. It started way back in 1992 with the topic of "Spirituality and Meaning of Life," again, through Robert Dilts with the contribution of Richard Bolstad and Connirae Andreas in 2014. It was then used by the International Association of NLP Institutes or IN-NLP.

NLPsy is the fourth and final movement in Neuro-linguistic Programming. In its mature form, it is called, "Neuro-linguistic Psychology" or NLPsy. It started in 2006 with the Research and Recognition Project. With its development by the International Association of NLP Institutes NLPsy has created the highest quality standard for trainers. The qualifications are stated as follows: Must have a master's degree in Psychology, a qualification for Psychotherapy on the level of the World Council for Psychotherapy, and an "NLP Master Trainer, IN" qualification. Not to mention the NLPsy Training which should be scientifically evaluated before and after each training.

Because of this, NLP has now been incorporated into sensory-based interventions and behavior-modification techniques designed to help clients improve their self-awareness, communication skills, confidence, and social actions. The current goal of NP in the field of Psychology is to help the client understand his thoughts, impulses, and behaviors deeper and to reframe these urges in a beneficial way towards healing and success.

To this day, NLP is incorporated into therapy to help patients with phobias, anxiety, poor self-esteem, stress, post-traumatic stress disorder, and many more. Psychotherapists also use this method to help a person reframe his thoughts in the midst of difficult situations to help them address their problems in an efficient and healthy way. With the help of a psychotherapist, NLP can be used to help clients understand and accept his own urges and drives to gain further control of it. They will start to understand why they think that way and why their behaviors manifest. NLP helps people to manage their moods, emotions, and predispositions. And when they do, they start to look at life from a more positive angle. People will start to see pas the negativities in life and begin in a more comfortable and satisfying mindset.

Empower your Mind Through Neuro-linguistic Programming

Learning the tricks of Neuro-linguistic Programming can help you utilize these thoughts and behaviors without the help of a psychotherapist. What if I told you that you could learn how to understand your deepest thoughts and emotions by learning NLP through this book? Isn't it amazing not to have to deal with stressful situations like you used to? When you start to learn about your mind and how it works, you can have full control over your impulses. Are you tired of seeing things negatively? Are you tired of all the frustration, the anxiety, and the fear that is brought to you by your own mind? Are you tired of the procrastinating, whining, and not getting things done? Well, my friend, this book is for you! Who said you could not be trained to control your own mind? I guarantee that by the end of this book, you will have an uncontrollable mindset towards success. All it takes is time, effort, and consistency. Read on to know more!

Neuro-linguistic Programming

From the term itself, Neuro-linguistic Programming is defined as the "language of your own mind." It creates the structure of your personality and explains the reason why you think that way, act that way, and speak that way. In all your years of living, NLP likened to be a memory unit where you store all your experiences and learnings. Whether these are conscious or unconscious information, it all helps build your unique personality and constructs your thoughts and behaviors.

Take a look at the software on your personal computers. The function, design, and amenities offered by these applications are defined by the code created by its programmers. This perfectly crafted software is not possible without the endless coding of computer scientists. It is constantly updated due to various innovations and developments. Hence, there is an unending improvement in the field of computer science. Much like this software and these applications, our brain decodes various inputs from the environment, embedding it like a code within the mind. In turn, it generates a predisposition, building a distinct personality for each person. This is the reason why we have individual differences. Our minds are coded differently from each other, so no person is exactly alike, not even identical twins. There will always be a difference in perception, preferences, skills, and talents. All because of Neuro-linguistic Programming.

We have also mentioned the constant need for development in the field of computer science. You would be surprised to know that the brain can do the same to its hard drive. Your psychological system aims to build a foundation of beliefs and attitudes for adaptation and self-preservation. Needless to say, the mind is a very resilient tool. You do not need to rely on techniques, steps, and tactics that have been taught to you over the years. Your brain is so powerful that it scours its network for ideas and new information you can use to cope with diversities and hardships. It allows you to learn new methods and techniques from scratch. It aims to redefine your program as needed for your own survival. So, even when you get stuck in a desert without anything at all, your brain will always figure something out. You just need to trust it.

Experts have created a brief saying about Neuro-linguistic Programming, "The conscious mind is the goal setter, and the unconscious mind is the goal-getter." A lot of people are so scared of letting their unconscious mind to get the best of them. To most people, they need to be conscious all the time – to be alert, to be sound and functional when deciding and solving problems. There is a reality in doing so to come up with better and reliable decisions. To be conscious means to rely on your awareness and learnings in the past. To be conscious means you need to recall everything – from your learnings to your training, and your interactions. What if you are faced by a problem that none of your experiences have taught you? There is nothing to think about nor to be conscious about because you have literally no idea what to do. So, how can you decide or solve a problem without any idea at all? You may use your conscious mind to recall every bit of information about this issue. But what if you are not aware of it at all?

This is where Neuro-linguistic Programming comes to aid. For example, you are in the midst of a very difficult exam. You were absent most of the time, and you have no idea what the contents of the exam mean. The more you try to think about the answers, the more you fail the exam. Note that there are things that happened in your life that you do not remember. It is embedded deep within your unconscious mind that only Neuro-linguistic Programming can reach. Even when you have no idea about the topics in the exam, stop stressing yourself out too much. You need to let your conscious mind rest and let your unconscious mind come to play. NLP allows you to connect every information you have gathered ever since you were a child. It establishes a connection or a pattern that allows you to find an answer to the questions.

Do you observe sometimes that even when you have absolutely no idea about a topic, somehow you manage to come up with an answer? In multiple choice questions, for example, when you are faced with difficult selections. Somehow, there is this one answer that looks familiar. It almost makes you feel like it is the correct one. There is a reason for these kinds of situations. You might have heard about the idea some time ago. You might have read it somewhere in a catalog, a magazine, or a pamphlet. Back then, it did not matter because it seemed so irrelevant. It was okay to forget. But your unconscious mind always remembers. Everything leaves an imprint inside your brain most of which the conscious mind cannot reach. That is the role of Neuro-linguistic Programming – to acquire the ability to unleash these hidden thoughts and emotions for a person's own self-preservation, a coping mechanism, and survival instincts.

In sports, on the other hand, why do you think the more an athlete thinks about the proper execution of movements, the more he fails to do it correctly. Neuro-linguistic Programming has already embedded these actions within your mind. It controls your muscle memory. The more you overthink an action, the more likely you are to fail because in your mind, there is doubt, fear, and worry. Neuro-linguistic Programming gets rid of all of that. All you need to do is trust your unconscious and let it go to work.

Neuro-linguistic Programming has many features that involve the psychological processes to influence behavior. It can provide efficient strategies, tactics, and methods so a person can form his attitude, belief, identity, and goals. It involved getting to know the whole program or brain system for awareness, and to gain control over these impulses, behaviors, and thoughts. All it takes is the right mindset to learn how.

Benefits of Neuro-linguistic Programming in 2019

1. It directs you towards success. No matter how hard life hits you, Neuro-linguistic Programming allows you to see these problems in a positive light. When you do, you eliminate your fear of failure and mistakes. You will feel more confident and determined to set goals and accomplish it one by one. The number one enemy of people who aspire success is fear and anxiety over their actions. Often, it is caused

by self-doubt. With the help of NLP, you can employ a personality, strong enough to withstand any circumstance and keep moving forward. It helps you to learn from your mistakes and apply these learnings in future decisions.

2. Improves communication and social interactions. Your unconscious says a lot. But you need to be able to unleash this information and ideas and put them in words. The goal of Neuro-linguistic Programming is to unleash the full potential of your subconscious in a positive way. In turn, you will be more confident in sharing your ideas in school or at the workplace. You are more confident to assert yourself in various situations to avoid frustration, loss, and depression.

3. It grants you control over your emotions, thoughts, and actions. When your emotional, psychological, and behavioral aspects are not in synchrony, there is a greater chance for internal conflict. You will be more stressed, less assertive, and more doubtful of yourself. You are less likely to create and achieve goals because your mind is hesitant to even when your heart feels determined. Sometimes, your body is capable, but your heart remains a skeptic. This cycle goes on and on until you reach the point of no return. By the time you realize you should have made better goals, it would be too late. Neuro-linguistic Programming helps you to unite these three components and make them work together towards a unified goal. With NLP, you will have a courageous mindset, a determined heart, and a strong body to tackle your daily problems.

4. Facilitates self-awareness. Knowing yourself from the inside out is a very important tool to reach your dreams in the future. You will be able to get to know your talents and skills which you can use to attain success. You will get to know your predispositions or tendencies, so you know what to control, what to improve, and what to avoid. Furthermore, you will get to know your personal triggers so that you can embrace your impulses and control it. All thanks to Neuro-linguistic Programming.

5. Supports weight loss. Two of the enemies of people who are overweight and obese are their poor eating habits and poor lifestyle. When these habits are ingrained deep within their thoughts, it makes it difficult for them to change their ways. No matter how much they try their best to lose weight, to employ a healthy diet and regular exercise, they cannot succeed without their ability to control their urges. Neuro-linguistic Programming helps a person commit to his goals and objectives in life. Through NLP, a person can have unstoppable self-discipline on the way to a successful weight loss.

6. Promotes learning. There are times when people get demotivated because they find it difficult to adjust to their lessons. They might feel depressed or frustrated because they do not understand any of what the teacher is saying. These situations cause anxiety and stress that might impact a person's learning capabilities. NLP can help reverse all these negativities and allows the mind to foster a positive thinking strategy to achieve learning goals.

7. Gets rid of bad habits. Neuro-linguistic Programming can be effective for drunkards and chain-smokers. It helps a person connect to his inner drives and control his impulses until he finally eliminates these habits.

8. Increases performance. There are times when a person becomes demotivated to work because he believes that he might perform poorly. This kind of negativity can be changed by Neuro-linguistic Programming. It helps a person access his deepest doubts and worry and redirect it to something productive. Experts have found that the use of NLP in the workplace has increased the workers' performance at a significant percentage. If you are having doubts about your capabilities, Neuro-linguistic Programming is the right tool for you.

Chapter 2

Mastery and body language

Everyone, to one extent or another, has one language in common—body language. Body language is subtle cues relayed by our body about our innermost thoughts, emotions, and intentions, and are often called non-verbal cues. Body language can show up in how we sit, stand, walk, and gesticulate. While our voice may say one thing, "Oh, I'm so happy!" our bodies can convey our true feelings—maybe you were not as happy as you claimed.

Nonverbal communication is much more important than most of us realize. It is one of the first forms of communication we experience, when we are infants. When we are newborns, we cannot communicate or understand speech. Our parents and caretakers understand this, and instead they cuddle us and make frequent eye contact in order to offer us communication through means we can understand. In addition, adults can pick up on how an infant might feel by how much they squirm and how much they smile. As adults, we also take more cues about others' emotions than we realize. For example, we may notice our friend seems to have her back turned toward us a rather large portion of the time on a particular day; perhaps she is slightly annoyed at you or feeling hostile. A woman may notice a man leaning in close to speak to her, suggesting that he is sexually attracted to her. Ever found yourself suddenly adjusting your clothing and hair in front of someone? You might have been nervous about impressing this person, whether you are going on an exciting first date or walking into a job interview.

Intuitively and unconsciously, most of us understand the importance of body language and how we can use it to our advantage. When we walk into a nightclub in a cool new outfit, we may walk with some extra spring in our step with our shoulders back and head up. We feel that we look good so we act accordingly to show others just how confident we feel. Sometime we lock eyes with a friend when someone else says something silly, sharing a moment of amusement. Body language is possibly one of the most forms of communication we as humans have.

Without body language, we would have serious difficulty understanding what other mean when they speak and would have a significantly harder time forming a first impression of some. While words can tell us where to be or what happened, body language conveys some of the most important information about the person we are talking to—whether or not they like us, feel attraction, hate us, are nervous, or are lying.

Nonverbal Cues Associated With Sitting

Sitting sounds like a fairly simple activity, which it is. The way we sit, however, can reveal quite a bit about ourselves. If you know what to watch out for in the way someone sits, you will have some insights about their mental and emotional state and how they actually feel about you.

Proximity

Have you ever had a nice cup of coffee on a bench with someone and realized how close they are sitting to you? They are leaning in to hear what you say and seem to have moved closer than they were in the beginning of the conversation. If someone is sitting close to you, this is a sign that they enjoy your company and want to feel close to you (either platonically or romantically). Sitting a little bit far however, or moving away when you move closer, suggests that they do not trust you very much or they do not particularly enjoy your company.

Legs Crossed

Plenty of people cross one leg over the other when the speak. When someone crosses their ankle over their knee and rests is on top, they are dominant and self-confident. In general, there are three body parts someone will expose if they are confident and relaxed; the belly button, the neck, and the crotch. These are vulnerable areas so if someone exposes them, they convey that they feel safe and secure. In contrast, crossing the legs at the ankles, locking them together, may indicate some shyness or apprehension. Crossing legs at the ankle is common in interview situations or when someone may be nervous, like meeting their partner's parents.

The most common way people cross their legs, one knee over the other, can go either way. If someone crosses their leg toward you, they are more likely to be fond of you and enjoy your company. Crossing a leg away from you can mean that they are uninterested in you sexually or want to create some distance between the two of you.

Tapping And Shaking Of The Feet

This is a classic example of fidgeting. Someone who is jiggling their leg on the ball of their foot or shaking their foot is most likely anxious or impatient. This is why we so often see this action during exams or in waiting rooms—they are both circumstances often full of expectations!

Legs Spread

Someone who sits with their legs spread is trying to be dominant. This position takes up quite a bit of space and opens up the bodies. If a man does it to a member of the preferred sex, it could also signal attraction, as he is exposing his crotch area to that person.

Nonverbal Cues Associated With The Arms

Ah yes, the arms! We use them to hug, wave at others, exercise, and dance. The arms are an interesting way our body can speak to others because they are almost like a gateway to our torso, which is a fairly vulnerable part of our bodies. With this in mind, the arms can convey all sorts of information about how a person feels and knowing what to watch out for can be very useful.

Arms Crossed

When someone has their arms crossed in front of them folded in front of their chest, be prepared for a possibly tense conversation. If you ask someone a question and they do this, they may be feeling stubborn, irritated, anxious, or insecure. They may also be trying to create emotional distance from you, putting up a barrier between yourself and the other person. Fear not though, sometimes, this gesture also means someone is thinking deeply about what you just said or asked, especially if the rest of their body language looks relatively relaxed.

One Or Both Hands On The Hips

Standing in this position often exudes dominance and confidence to the point of hostility or aggression. The pointy elbows serving as a barrier to the torso almost scream, "don't come any closer!" Someone who stands with a hand or two on the hips may be trying to come off as confident and independent—why else would fashion models use this pose so often?

Waving The Arms While Speaking

This gesture can go in either direction, emotionally speaking. Someone may wave their arms and wring their hands in either aggravation or excitement. With that said, the person doing this is either very aggravated or very excited.

Nonverbal Expressions Associated With Fingers And Hand Gestures

We use our hands and fingers for just about anything requiring precision and attention to detail. The hands can grab small objects and move the finger to point at things we see. Babies first experience their own agency through their fingers and hands, just look at strong their little grasp can be!

The Handshake

Let's introduce ourselves—most people would reach their hand out to grasp the other person's and hold it firmly, trying not to be uncomfortably tight while also trying not to hold so loosely that shyness or aloofness is conveyed. In general, someone initiating a handshake with you is a sign of warmth and friendliness. They want to get to know you and look forward to speaking more.

Touching The Nose

Sometimes when you ask a question, someone who is lying may begin touching their nose. This may seem random, but there's some biology facts that back up why this happens. When people lie, the body releases chemicals that cause some of the blood to rush to our face. This can cause some itching of the slightest bit of tingling, and anyone tends to touch areas that feel this way. The liar will not only realize they are doing but also not even register that they have a little itch on their nose.

Hands Behind The Back

The most obvious quality of this pose is how vulnerable it leaves the torso. If someone allows for such vulnerability, take note. Having the hands behind the back can signal submission to another person. On the flip side however, it can also convey confidence, as leaving the torso so vulnerable suggests that someone trusts that they will not be hurt.

Exposing the Palms

Exposing the palms and wrists is a way of exposing oneself. Just think of how sensitive the palms are and how many delicate veins are in the awrist. Exposing these areas conveys more trust and openness than you may realize. If someone expose their wrists and palms to you, they are communicating openness and trustworthiness. By exposing the palms, someone is unconsciously showing you that they have nothing to hide.

Clasping And Fidgeting With Hands

The person who is clasping their hands, rubbing them together, and fidgeting with their own fingers may need a hug. This is a self-pacifying action, meaning that it is an attempt to calm down and relax. Someone who does this may be in distress, anxious, or afraid of something. If you see someone doing this, be friendly to them—they may need it more than they want you to know.

Nonverbal Gestures Of The Head

The face and head possibly convey the heart of our emotions. There is a lot more than a grain of truth to the saying that goes, "they eyes are the windows to the soul." We can tell someone's emotions and interest in what we are saying based on their facial expressions and their physical orientation toward us.

Nodding Up And Down

When someone nods up and down, this signals approval or agreement about whatever you may be saying. If accompanied by eye contact, the person is meaning to convey that they are paying close attention to what you are saying. In general, this is a good sign; someone who listens is being polite and giving you the time and attention that you deserve during an interaction.

Raised Eyebrows

Raised eyebrows are a sign of interest, sexual or otherwise. If someone's eyebrows raise slightly when they see you, there is a good chance they have the hots for you. If it is a friend or more platonic relationship who does this while you are speaking, they could be expressing surprise or shock. Think of it this way—by raising the eyebrows, they are opening the eyes up more, almost as if to show you something in themselves (attraction) or to take in more information (like what you are saying and showing).

The Closed Smile

A big, toothy smile signals genuine happiness and agreeability, but what about the tight, closed-mouth smile? This type of smile is a little bit less happy. Someone smiling like this may be trying to hide something or may be faking a friendly smile for appearances' sake. Think about having to say hi to someone you do not particularly like; you want to be polite, but it is hard to bring yourself to do so. You may have unconsciously given this person a smile with your mouth closed to be friendly without revealing to much about yourself.

Microexpressions

A microexpression is an ultrafast display of a particular emotion that flashes across someone's face. It is so quick that an untrained observer is usually unable to catch it. Even the person who exhibited the microexpression is unaware that they did it. The seven universal microexpressions are contempt, disgust, happiness, surprise, anger, sadness, and fear. These expressions are so primal that they are expressed the same across people no matter where on earth they were raised. An Inuit person's microexpressions will look identical to those of an American person or a Japanese person's or a Haitian person's.

Body Language And Attraction

Very rarely do we find out someone is attracted to us based on their words, at least initially. Sometimes we just walk away from a conversation with a feeling that this conversation was somehow a little bit more flirtatious than most. Perhaps the person made more eye contact than usual or touched our arm at some point.

We often have trouble ascertaining whether someone is interested in us romantically or sexually because some many body language cues can be easy to miss, and we are often unsure of ourselves in romantic situations. With that said, men and women may express attraction through their body language very differently and knowing how the two genders express themselves sexually can be useful and clear up a lot of confusion.

How Women Display Attraction

Often, when women display attraction to you, they do so by showing off the most feminine parts of their body. Keep this in mind when you are scratching your head wondering whether she likes you.

Touching Her Hair

This is the classic movie moment where the male protagonist is gazing into his crush's eyes while having a mundane conversation with her and she tucks some hair behind her ears or twirls a little bit around her fingers. She may also toss her hair behind her shoulder. She does this to draw attention to a feminine part of herself and also as an unconscious grooming technique to look her best for you.

Standing At Attention

this is a woman's sexiest posture, and she is most definitely doing it on purpose. What does it look like? It is all in the arch of her back. When a woman arches her back, she is showing off her breasts and buttocks, making them appear prominent, larger, and perkier. She is doing this to get your attention and show off the goods. Enjoy the view, then go ask her if you can buy her a drink.

Touching Herself

When a woman rubs her neck, shoulders, or legs in your presence, consider yourself lucky! These gestures are an invitation to intimacy sometimes. By rubbing these areas on her body, she is unconsciously suggesting she wants you to touch her too. With that said, do not proceed to pounce on this poor woman. Instead, take these gestures as a small invitation to come closer and get into her space. She will appreciate you taking it slow.

The Gaze

Is she looking at you a lot, and then looking away? If she returns your gaze and holds it when your eyes meet, there is a good chance she is intrigued. Prolonged eye contact between two people is an intense and vulnerable moment. For most people, such a look conveys either aggression and intimidation or attraction. If she keeps looking at you and does not seem to mind all the eye contact, she wants you to initiate contact.

Clothing Adjustment

This one is cute. If she keeps touching her jewelry and adjusting her clothes, especially in ways that expose her body more, she wants to expose more of herself to you. For example, rolling up her sleeves or removing her sweater, even if the room is cold, are signs she wants you to see more of her body. In addition, if it seems like she is fidgeting with her clothes and continuously readjusting, she is engaging in some grooming to make herself as attractive as possible for you.

How Men Display Attraction

Fear not! Men certainly communicate with their bodies too, but in ways that are more assertive than women. Men will often use physical displays of dominance to display their attraction to you. Most male body language of attraction is an unconscious signal of strength and power, unlike women who tend to draw attention to characteristics of their beauty. Next time you want to know whether you should talk to that guy across the bar, think about these tips before shooting your shot.

Foot Position

If a guy is interested in you, he will want to angle himself towards you in one way or another. If his body or face are not turned at you but his feet are, that's a good sign. If he likes you, he will angle his feet in your direction to signal interest.

He Is Comfortable Touching You

Picture yourself on a bench with your cutie when your knees accidentally touch. Does he pull away or let them stay there, continuing to touch? If it is the latter, congratulations! He likes you and craves your touch. He is comfortable enough to have you in his personal space.

Showing Off The Package

This is quite the move. It occurs when a guy stand confident, legs slightly apart, with his thumbs resting in his belt loops or his hands in a similar area. By doing this, he is showing off the goods and showing a more sexual side of himself, drawing attention to his sexual organ.

Preening

Men and women have this in common actually! Like women, men will also unconsciously adjust and fidget with their clothing in order to look their best.

Touching You

Men are sometimes a bit more forward than women when it comes to initiating touch. If he is into you, he may touch your back, shoulder, or knee (if you seem comfortable already). By breaking the touch barrier, he is making it clear that he wants you in his personal space and is thinking about touching you even more later. With that said, if he goes straight for grabbing your but, run away! This man may lack boundaries or feel ownership over you if he gropes you too early.

Looking You In The Eyes

Once again, men tend to be a little bit more aggressive than women when it comes to body language and attraction. Unlike women, who may look towards their interest and then look away, men will attempt to hold prolonged eye contact. They will also check out your body, moving their eyes up and down to more thoroughly drink in the sight of you.

Chapter 3

Persuasion: How To Influence People With NLP Techniques.

To develop the ability to communicate persuasively, you first need to understand the key persuasive language principles. This section highlights those principles, and seeks to help you understand the key elements you need to work on to improve your persuasion skills.

True And Lasting Influence Occurs In The Subconscious Mind

To master persuasive language, the key principle you need to comprehend is that lasting and true influence occurs only on the level of your subconscious mind and not in your conscious mind.

Your subconscious mind is a gigantic memory bank with an unlimited capacity. It stores all the little and big information related to everything that happens to you. Your subconscious mind is in charge of storing and retrieving data and ensuring you respond in an appropriate manner. Your subconscious makes everything you do and say fit a pattern consistent with your master program and your self-concept.

Your subconscious is also subjective and does not reason or think independently. It obeys commands given by the conscious mind. The conscious mind works as a gardener that plants seeds in your subconscious mind, which serves as a garden wherein the planted seeds germinate and then grow.

Your conscious mind directs your subconscious to behave a certain way and your subconscious merely obeys it. While your conscious mind does command your subconscious, the subconscious mind holds all the power because it stores all data. Hence, to persuade and convince someone, you have to appeal to the person's subconscious mind.

Your conscious mind communicates using concrete thoughts and logic. Conversely, your subconscious mind communicates via feelings, emotions, and intuition. To persuade your husband to buy you a new car, using facts, figures, and logical data will not help you connect with him nor will it persuade him.

Instead, you should target his subconscious mind and use emotions and sentiments. You can do this by telling him how amazing he is and how you are glad he prioritizes; then, you will indirectly bring up the topic of purchasing a new car.

Similarly, if you want your boss to give you a raise, you will use the emotional element to convince him/her. You will focus on how much value you bring to the company instead of using logic to make your case that you deserve a raise. This tactic will help you easily accomplish your goal since humans are creatures of emotions.

Human Beings are Creatures of Emotion

Dale Carnegie's meaningful quote clearly explains the following: to persuade humans, you have to target their emotions. To persuade someone, you have to focus on emotions while at the same time, maintaining a balance between feelings and logic. Logic and emotions are the keys to persuade anyone. As such, tactfully convincing your listeners means you have to strike a balance between them.

Emotions create action, movement, and energy. A logic driven conversation may seem boring, but by adding the right amount of emotions to it, you can instantly spice it up and effectively get your message across.

However, if your conversation is devoid of logic, it may not appeal to intelligent listeners. This is why it is important to maintain balance between emotions and logic: so you can appeal to all sorts of audience, those whose sway lies in emotion, and those whose sway is reason. This skill is what this book shall teach you.

Subtlety is the Way to Persuade People

Everyone has in their mind something called the critical faculty. The critical faculty acts kind of like a computer firewall; it filters ideas based on logic and reasoning. It is designed to protect us from harmful or incorrect information by allowing us to choose which information we would like to accept and which information is not good for us and should be rejected. However, it is also the biggest obstacle we face when trying to persuade someone, help them to see past their limitations, or guide them towards a new point of view.

In persuasion, the goal is to communicate with someone's subconscious mind without any objections, and get past this critical faculty. To bypass that person's critical thinking, you must add subtlety to your speech.

Subtlety refers to communicating your message in an effective, firm, and gentle manner. In order to get someone to see things our way, we don't want to have a battle of wits or try to prove someone as being factually wrong; in fact quite the opposite. Doing this will not help you persuade people. Rather, it will cause people to dislike you. Instead, we want to use suggestions and triggers to access their subconscious directly, in order to guide them gently to our point of view.

To sway people without hurting their feelings, you have to add subtlety to your speech, which is where emotions come in. Subtlety helps you use triggers and suggestions to access a person's subconscious mind and steer them gently towards your viewpoint.

Imagine you are working with a team on a project and you notice a good way to direct the project. However, you fear your idea may displease the group leader because it contradicts with the group leader's idea.

Here, to prove your point, you could reason with the group leader but you fear this strategy may alienate you from the group. However, since you feel your idea has a greater chance of success, you decide to use emotions to persuade the group leader.

You gently approach the group leader and compliment him or her on the good job he or she is doing directing the team. This instantly cheers the group leader who ends up liking you. Then, you cleverly enforce the need to work in the company's and project's best interests.

Once the group leader agrees to your notion, you steer the conversation towards your idea by stating you read it somewhere. By appealing to the leader's emotions, you gently direct his or her attention towards your idea without offending him or her.

As you can see, subtlety and emotions help you sway people. In this book, we will uncover many strategies that help you tap into people's subconscious and influence them in the most effective way possible.

By now, you've learned about the basics of NLP, subliminal persuasion, cold reading, and different aspects of analysis that you can use to understand and get to know people without interacting with them directly. Now, the question is, how can you really use these skills to manipulate them into doing your bidding? Well, there are many different ways that incorporate all of these skills without ethical or moral risk to yourself. This chapter explains different tricks to really persuade another that will incorporate everything you have learned from this book. There are different ways you can approach a situation, and each one calls for a different tactic or approach. It's important to know multiple ways of persuading others, and examples of these situations are provided in this chapter. However, it is important to remember these rules that apply to every persuasive trick.

Be Observant

You can't get anywhere if you don't pay attention to your surroundings, the situation, or, most importantly, the person you are trying to persuade. Mood, behavior, and the situation must be appropriate for the moment for the trick to be affective. Remember how to read body language and know how to read this person before you attempt to manipulate them into anything. For example, in one tactic that will be described in this chapter, the key to success is to keep the person focused on the conversation. If you aren't paying attention for the passion and attention needed to make the trick work, you will be caught and your success is unlikely. Attention and observation is key to manipulation.

Honesty and Trustworthiness

No one is going to follow the advice or suggestion of someone they don't trust. Even if the situation doesn't call for rapport or a pre-developed relationship, you need to appear trustworthy. Remember the indicators of discomfort and lying when it comes to body language and avoid them when speaking. If you're telling a half truth or even lying to get what you want from someone, you can't do so while holding your hands behind your back and shifting your weight from one foot to the other. If you can, be genuinely honest, especially if the other person won't expect it. If you seem trustworthy and reliable, people will respond accordingly.

Now that you know all you need to for success, listed below are different examples of how you can persuade someone to do what you want. These techniques range from small favors to large ideas, and each has been drawn from a different source. You'll have a tactic for each occasion, and if you follow the rules listed above and remember all of the knowledge you've gained in this book, you will be successful and gain every advantage you need to get what you desire.

Oversell Your Idea

An NLP tactic used often in the sales industry is to use intense passion to hype-up the idea you want to sell someone on. It's a common practice seen by anyone trying to sell a product, and it works. I've been roped into buying something I regretted many times based entirely on the sales technique. I'm still upset that that skin cream didn't give me perfect skin. When you exaggerate the benefits of an idea and put emphasis on the main points that could sell it, your logic seems sound and it's hard to argue. If someone doesn't really need something, don't tell them that they need it, explain why they need it. Don't even go near the idea of giving them the option. If you want someone to donate to your favorite organization, tell them how doing so will benefit them just as much as it will help benefitting the organization itself. Set them up for following through before they even know what it is you want to propose. This technique works well when you want someone to take something, which is why it is taught to all sales clerks and is used in advertisements. It also works well with the opposite technique, which is oversimplifying the idea.

Oversimplify Your Idea

If the idea is complicated and contains drawbacks, it might benefit you to oversimplify it. Oversimplification, by definition, is to leave out information and simplify what you do include until it is distorted. To do this in persuasion, you adjust what you should explain when it comes to your idea. If you want someone to take martial arts lessons with you, but you know that they don't care much for bumps and bruises, you could try this technique. Describe the benefits of learning a martial art. You could explain how you'll both be more active and fit, you'll have the means to defend yourself in an emergency, and you'll learn moves to show off should the occasion arise. Maybe offer to show a few videos of successful martial arts techniques that are visually appealing. If you use enough passion when selling your points, the idea of minor injury might not even occur to your friend. Though, in the case of this example, they might not thank you for it later.

Put Yourself in a Neutral Position

If possible, maintain the illusion of neutrality and limit any perceived bias. For example, if your friend's girlfriend had been begging him to cut his hair for a while, so he looks to you for a second opinion, you shouldn't express any real interest. If you have a quarrel with his hair length, you might say that either way it doesn't matter to you, however, the length indicated in his girlfriend's picture would frame his face well, and in the coming hot weather it will prevent possible heat stroke. Using words with specific reactions helps. In this case, the word "however" leads people to focus more on what was said after than what was said before. By bringing in logical points and behaving as if your opinion was completely without motive, your friend will likely opt for the haircut, and his girlfriend may even owe you a favor.

Change the Environment to Your Advantage

Studies have shown that the environment someone is in can have an impact on their decisions. This would come as a form of subliminal persuasion. For example, if you desperately need a study partner for an upcoming exam, you shouldn't ask your preferred partner in the mall. The mall is surrounded by fun activities, bright lights, music, and other distractions. However, if you were to ask him in an environment that stimulates the idea of studying in his brain, such as the library, he's more likely to agree with you. Better yet, if you can somehow work a pencil and a textbook into the atmosphere, you'll almost guarantee to win over his answer. Studies have shown that the brain works differently in different environments, which is why it can be difficult to recognize a co-worker or peer in a supermarket. If you want someone to make a business transaction, your success is more likely if there is a briefcase and a fountain pen within their vision, as these items tend to bring out the desire for money in people.

Speak Quickly

If you find yourself caught in an argument that you plan to win, speed up your speech. If you're speaking quickly, you sound more prepared with arguments, and your opponent has far less time to think of a coherent response, as he or she is focused on processing your arguments instead. The other person will become flustered in their confusion and trip up on their arguments. Eventually they will drop their side of the disagreement out of frustration and you will come out victorious. Watch for signs of irritation and frustration on their face. If you see these signs, you are close to winning.

Butter Them Up Ahead of Time

If you use subliminal persuasion and NLP to provide ideas that someone should do something or is excelled in a certain area you need them to be, they'll believe it. If you do this ahead of time, when the time comes for you to ask that favor or propose the idea, they will want to follow through. Remember the rules of subliminal persuasion, however. The ideas shouldn't appear to come from you. Point out objects that may put the idea in their head, or, play your reaction to awe whenever the idea of them doing the act is brought up. For example, if you want someone to paint your living room, you might steer them towards a creative environment and draw attention to a paint roller. You could pick it up and observe it, stand near it a moment, or even look at it for an extended length of time. If they take interest in the object, such as picking it up or looking at it thoughtfully, focus your reaction. Act interested in the idea of them painting a wall. Then, when you actually put in the request, refer to that moment and explain why you think they are perfect for the job. Environment, body language analysis, and subliminal persuasion all come into play here.

When in Doubt, Collect a Favor

The easiest way to ask for a favor, is to provide one beforehand. If you aid someone's success in some way, or bail them out of a tough situation, they'll feel inclined to return this act of kindness later. If you've been painting yourself as an honest, genuine person as described in the tactic of NLP, the act will feel genuine. Those who have been given something from a generous person always feel the obligation to return the favor. It is best, however, to incorporate subliminal persuasion, and not to outright say that they owe you a favor. Nothing makes a kind act seem more benevolent than a selfless one without reciprocation. For example, you could begin the statement with, "Will you do me a favor?" Instead of outright asking them to do the favor. Because of the previous favor or favors you have done for them, they will answer before they even know what it is. This trick is especially useful if you believe they won't enjoy the request.

Shock Them

This can be done in multiple ways. One way to shock a person into complying, is to display what you know, or maybe what you don't, about them. This is an excellent chance to try out some cold reading and display your analysis skills. If you know a lot about someone, you must have paid attention and genuinely care. If you do this, and don't give the other time to think about the action that just occurred, they'll likely do as you suggest without an after-thought. Don't use this tactic often, however, as a shocking act isn't so shocking if it's done multiple times. As an example, you could surprise them with their favorite meal or make a comment on an interest of theirs that they mentioned in passing at one time.

Blackmail Exists

Often a desperate act that will likely lose the confidence you've built in someone is blackmail. Because it is so risky, and displays a mean streak, it is best to avoid blackmail all together. However, if you absolutely must, you have the skills to do so effectively. With cold reading, you can pull information from the person you wish to blackmail. An odd smudge of lipstick on your male friend's face, a lie you overheard someone speak that you could threaten to share or using a vague statement about something they could have did that you know nothing about, while allowing them to fill in the gaps and "realize" what you mean. These same tricks can be used under the category of earning a favor, however. You could hint that you noticed that lipstick or heard that lie, and promise you'll keep their secrets. You could also use the same trick of hinting you know what you really don't in this same way. Not only will you maintain the relationship you need to gain further favors from this person, but you won't earn a nasty reputation that could prevent further manipulation of other people. Remember, an important aspect of persuasion is to appear trustworthy.

What People do Subconsciously

A simple trick that I've personally used is to distract someone while you guide them to do something. These acts must be simple, and you'll need a little muscle memory on the other person's part. You could engage them in a conversation about something they are passionate about or interested in. Remain engaged in this conversation and keep them going. If you want them to hold something, open a door, or perform another simple task, you can guide them to the act while keeping the conversation going. Without realizing it, your companion will do as you wish subconsciously. It may not be an extravagant manipulation, but it can make your life simpler if you've gone shopping with this person and want them to carry the bags or want them to hold onto your coffee. Guiding them to the act has to remain subtle, as their focus must remain on the conversation. By the time they realize what has happened, the act is usually over, if they notice at all. For example, I know someone who has more passion about a video game in his little finger than most people have in their whole bodies for anything else. Walking to his house, I didn't feel like holding the bag I had taken with me. I casually brought up the conversation of this game and watched his eyes light up. His head became taller and his stance was more relaxed. As he began talking, I asked a few questions to keep him moving along. I watched for the opportunity when his hand extended to me while he explained a concept to me and I handed it to him. He didn't seem to notice as he continued describing a fictional race of elves with enthusiasm. He simply continued to hold the bag as he spoke all the way to his house. Had I asked him to hold my bag without using persuasion, he might have still done so, but there's still that chance that he wouldn't.

Switch it up

Switching up both word choices and sentence length will increase your chances of getting a "yes" for the request you are asking. Using "I" phrases instead of "you" phrases or "don't" instead of "can't" lead the person you're requesting to come to the conclusion themselves. This is a form of subliminal persuasion, as you don't outright ask what you want. For example, the sentence "Will you go to the department store?" Doesn't sound as appealing as "I am so exhausted, and I still have to go to the department store". If you play the victim and appear in need of aid, the other person might come to your rescue. This is especially true if you've done a favor for them recently. Switching up sentence length is both an author trick and a speaker trick as well to keep an audience engaged. If you alternate between long and brief sentences, your statement sounds more appealing to the ear, and you sound more certain. Authors will change up sentence lengths when describing a scene to give readers a break from the long sentences for a moment. It's difficult to follow a large block of word, even if it's spoken. It is also important to use appealing word descriptions instead of simple phrases. Convincing someone to eat organic foods is more possible if you use words such as "all natural" instead of the simple "healthy". This is why advertisements exclaim, usually in large letters, loaded descriptions of their product.

Mimic Body Language

When someone sees familiarity in you, even at a subconscious level, they'll respond more positively to your requests. You can mirror a person's body language while using any other technique as well, so it may act as that cherry on top that will get you what you want. For example, if you have developed the needed rapport with this person, have set the environment as you need to, and yet you still feel like you need one extra push to drive the idea home for them, watch their movement and study the way they move. Do they toss their hair out of their eyes? Maybe they roll their shoulders often. Have they uncrossed and re-crossed their legs multiple times? Small movements that they don't realize they are doing should be the key focus when you copy their body language. If they see something of themselves in you, at a subconscious level, they will trust you more and will be more open to your suggestions.

Pay Attention

This may seem like an idea that's too simple, however it pays to pay attention to someone. If you've just listened to what the other person is saying and used your own body language to show that you were listening and interested just before you make your request, you are more likely to persuade them. People want to be heard. If they feel like you have listened and genuinely care about what they have to say, they'll be more responsive to you. You can do this by facing them with your body as they speak and make eye contact with them. Nod at appropriate times and ask questions. It's important to put your analysis skills to work in this moment as well. Are they responding positively to your efforts? Do they appear to be engaged in the conversation? Is their mood appropriate for the request? It won't work to your advantage to ask a favor of someone who has just told you about their favorite cat passing away. Keep the conversation light, but make sure the other person is engaged and cares about what they are saying.

Take Advantage of Confusion

Humans are habitual creatures. By nature, we all tend to follow some sort of routine, and when it falters, we scramble. When this happens, a person tends to cling to the closest action they can take in the midst of their confusion. If this has happened, and the person is a bit lost, you can take advantage of the moment to suggest a course of action that is preferable to you. They'll likely take any sort of direction they can get to go back on track, so they'll take the suggestion more easily than if they were clear-minded. Here is an example of this persuasive technique. Your friend always goes to a specific restaurant for lunch on Friday. This Friday, she has asked that you join her to catch up. You don't care much for the menu, and the last time you dined there you felt ill that night. However, your friend is adamant and you're both on your way. Luckily, she also drives the same direction to this restaurant every Friday. Today, there's an unexpected detour due to construction and your friend is visibly shocked. Now would be the time to suggest a different place. Speak calmly and suggest somewhere you can navigate to under these new circumstances. Your friend will oblige to escape the mess of confusion she's found herself in. You'll get your choice of restaurant, and your friend will thank you for being so helpful.

Lying

When using lying as a persuasive technique, it is best not to do so with someone who you have been building a relationship with. Lying is best used on someone whom you haven't built the basic NLP foundations with and likely never will. The reason is, those who know your baseline reaction and body language can spot the anxious behaviors of a lie much more easily than someone who has just met you. When lying, you'll need to utilize your cold reading and analysis skills more than NLP or subliminal persuasion, as these skills can be used from afar. Pay attention to their behavior and watch for their reactions. Is there suspicion written in their eyes? This can be seen as tension in the forehead, pursed lips, and slightly narrowed eyes. If they seem to believe your story, their face will hold interest. They won't be fidgeting and they might occasionally nod. It's important to pay attention to your own body language as well. Remember, when someone is leaning away from another, they are perceived as uncomfortable, and if they are hiding their hands in any way, they are hiding something. Try not to touch your hands together or hide them and keep your perceived mood light.

The Ellsberg Paradox

Known for leaking the Pentagon Papers, Daniel Ellsberg began his career by studying decision-making. His paradox is explained with an example of two urns. The first urn is full of black and red balls of an unknown ratio. There could be one black ball and the rest are red, it could be 50 of one and 50 of the other, no one knew. The second urn was, for certain, 50 of one and 50 of the other. People were asked to guess which color they would draw before choosing which urn to draw from. Anyone who drew they guess would win $100 and anyone who guessed incorrectly would get nothing. What Ellsberg discovered was that most of the population chose to bet before drawing from the known urn.

What this explains, is that people tend to avoid risks. If you present a choice to someone, and provide all of the facts of one, and admit to some unknown factors to the other, they will likely choose the option that is complete, regardless of the facts. You can use this to your advantage if you want to sway their decision one way or another. A little deception and oversimplifying may be included in this tactic, so it is important to remember your body language and how it is perceived to the other person.

Group Influence

There is a reason companies will display their top reviews in a visible space on their website. People often base their decisions on statistics, even if it is a statistic based solely on the opinions of others and no science or evidence. If a group or people are willing to agree with you, that last person you are trying to persuade is likely to change their stance to match up with the majority vote. You can do this in a variety of ways, from persuading the others individually, or choosing people you already know will agree with you to back up your idea. Just as a group of sheep will follow each other, humans can fall into the group complex as well.

Present You High Selling Points First

In any situation, people tend to focus on the information they were given first the most. This is why gossip is frowned upon, as people are likely to believe the false rumors more than the facts, even if they were presented after. If the first point on your idea is a weak one, the other person may not follow through, even if the following points are logical and strong. Think about your word choice, and word order carefully before you present the idea. Use your other skills to ensure this person is open to a new idea and drive it home by offering the greatest benefits from the beginning. They will focus on that and are more likely to agree with you. This trick is best mixed with others, such as the favor exchange, the group complex, or overselling your idea.

Contrast Your Requests

Sometimes, if your request is large and will likely be difficult to persuade someone on, you can begin by making a smaller one in advance. If you ask someone to help you with a minor thing, such as making a run to the store for you, they may do so. After, you can ease your way up to the larger request you originally wanted to make, such as keeping a big secret for you or taking a big risk. Inversely, you can also make a small request seem simple and logical by first proposing a grand, likely ridiculous scheme. You could begin with something outrageous like streaking through a store or performing a grand heist. After your large idea is shot down, you can then attempt the smaller, less risky favor. Because the first one seemed beyond logical reasoning, the second option will appear reasonable in comparison, and the other person will be more inclined to comply. Stores and online shops use this trick in the form of a decoy sale. They may offer three options of a product. One is decently priced, the second is expensive, and the third is a combination of the two at the same price as the expensive option. Which one is the decoy? The expensive option is placed to increase the appeal of the third choice, making it look like a deal that it might not have seemed like before. Another version of this trick is when shops frequently have "sales" which actually contain the real price, with a much larger version of the price set as the original value. Who hasn't been a victim of this manipulation? It's hard to say no to a pack of fourteen pairs of socks when they are ten dollars off for a limited time.

Limited Time

Another tactic companies use that you can experiment with, is the limited time trick. It's hard to pass up something that states it only exists for a limited time, as the stress of never having such an opportunity again puts pressure on you. You can use this to your advantage and offer an opportunity to your friend as a chance that won't come again. For example, if you'd like your co-worker to call in sick on the same day as you, you might look up events that are happening on that day. If that co-worker refuses, or seems hesitant to join you, you can explain that there is a concert of only local bands playing at the park that day and they may never play again. Neither of you may be especially fond of local bands, however the fact that they may not come again will at least give your co-worker pause. If you can find a time sensitive occasion that appeals to the other person, you're even more likely to get what you want out of them. The more they hesitate before responding, the more they are considering the option. Remember, it is also beneficial to begin with the selling points. So, don't begin your request with, "I know we might get fired, but let's skip work tomorrow!"

The "But You're Free" Technique

People like choices. Having the freedom to choose between different options, or to not opt for an option at all, make them feel more in control of a situation and more likely to agree. If you wish to sway someone to do something specific, you may present it as an option. Use your other skills and sell the idea. Make is sound plausible and apply how it will benefit the other person just as much, or more than you. Watch their reactions and see if you have caught their interest. If all goes well, then you can drive the idea home by using a magic statement at the end. "But you're free not to". As it is a choice option, people will respond more positively and will often opt to perform the action based on the fact that they have the choice. Of course, they likely had the choice to begin with. This is why psychology works so well, because the brain and mind can be tricked.

Use a Relatable Experience

Sometimes, people want reassurance that they aren't alone in a situation. If you provide some common ground and explain an anecdote that is relatable to the situation that has a positive outcome, the other person is more inclined to agree to follow through with theirs. If you are pushing someone to take a risky job, explain a time when you took a risk and how it benefited you. Success stories drive a lot of people to take chances. Remember, people don't like to take risks about the unknown. So, provide them with information to base their decision on.

It Worked Before, It'll Work Again

Many people believe that if something worked well in their favor, the streak will continue on. Gambling is a business that preys on this belief, as people who are lucky enough to win at a game will lose all of their winnings on pushing that luck and playing again. You can use it to your advantage as well, especially if you want someone to do something that they, or another person, has attempted before with success. If you remind this person that the previous situation was favorable, they are more likely to comply with your logic. Of course, if this action was based on luck, such as the gambling is, the chances of it turning out as favorable has no correlation with the previous outcome. However, the other person may not know that fact, as many don't.

Chapter 4

Manipulation

We have discussed that Neuro-linguistic Programming is very effective when somebody chooses a life-changing path. In doing so, one needs to be able to manipulate his mind to gain control over his impulses, drives, thoughts, feelings, and behavior. When people think about manipulation, it often elicits a very negative approach. Reasonable enough, some people use manipulation to acquire their selfish needs. But in this chapter, I will be discussing the value of ethical manipulation. That is the manner of converting negative energy into a positive drive through the physical, emotional, mental, and spiritual aspects of the human being persona.

Why is there a need for ethical manipulation? Simply put, all of us are born perfectly. However, we are born in a very chaotic and very cruel world. We are all born in a difficult life. Rich or poor. Man or woman. We all experience hardships from time to time. These negative experiences shape our minds and hearts in a way that is undesirable. We start to learn how to lie, to steal, to procrastinate, and to lose faith just to survive or withstand pressure. Because of these, we become accustomed to bad lifestyles and habits that are detrimental in achieving our goals. Life gives us fear, self-doubt, anxiety, pressure, and depression. From our experiences, we have learned to be pessimistic rather than optimistic. We started to become too critical, too selfish, too skeptic about everything. Hence, we do not really know what we want from life. All we think about is keeping up with the expectations of society even when we are not happy about it. Most of us die without experiencing even the tiniest bit of happiness. They think they know what they are doing. They think they are contented. But actually, they have other things in mind they just cannot fathom.

See, people let themselves stay limited in their actions, thoughts, beliefs, and aspirations. They have no idea that there is more than what they can learn from their environment. The choices they have now does not even reach half of what they can do. The skillset and talents they think they can do perfectly are not even remote to their full potential

This is the beauty of Neuro-linguistic Programming and Ethical Manipulation. It allows a person to unleash everything from their conscious to their subconscious. It frees the mind and clears it to be able to see countless ways and techniques to live life. Neuro-linguistic Programming breaks away the chains that tether us to the demands of society. It makes us spontaneous, bold, relentless, and successful. The only question left for us is how.

Ethical manipulation does is driven by achievement and rewards. It has four major objectives, namely:

To Influence. Ethical manipulation is geared toward making a person see things from a different perspective. It makes a person to do something that they are not naturally inclined to do. For example, a chain smoker or an alcoholic has the least tendency to give up their vices because they believe that they cannot live without their bad habits. To influence this person, you need to make them see things in a different light. This pushes him to give up his faulty behaviors and change his ways. We have discussed that the duration is necessary for Neuro-linguistic Programming to work. With the help of ethical manipulation, it prepares the person of what is to come in the road to a life-changing path.

To Persuade. To persuade means to adopt a certain way of thinking. This is applicable to people who have a phobia, anxiety, and depression. Ethical manipulation can help individuals to see things positively to elicit functional behaviors and redefine self-defeating thoughts.

To Inspire. Ethical manipulation is also used to motivate the person towards success. Whether it is weight loss or financial gain, Neuro-linguistic Programming matched with ethical manipulation is effective to keep a person determined in doing his best.

To Unify. We have discussed that the congruence between the mind and the body is an important factor in achieving goals. Ethical manipulation helps a person achieve that coherence by facilitating a clear mindset and perception in making decisions and solving problems. It eliminates fear and self-doubt. Ethical manipulation allows a person to know what he really wants and how he wants to accomplish it.

Methods of Manipulation

Psychiatrists use these forms of ethical manipulation to help their clients improve their ways of thinking. To some people, they use these methods in a negative manner; in Neuro-linguistic Programming, these methods of manipulation are done for the welfare of the client. With practice and discipline, you can manipulate your mind as well while using several forms of positive manipulation.

1. Positive Reinforcement. This includes praising yourself and rewarding yourself after every positive deed. When your mind is wired to think that there is something positive out of what you're doing, even by just accomplishing short-term goals, it will be inclined to double its efforts towards positive.

2. Denial. One of the simplest ways to manipulate the mind is through denial. It is not that kind of denial where you deny a stressful situation. Denial through ethical manipulation means to deny yourself of the pleasures that puts your integrity and health in vain. This includes denying yourself of fatty foods and junk foods when you aim to lose weight. It includes denying yourself of all the vices you wish to get rid of. No matter how hard it is in the beginning, your mind will start to accustom to this change. Soon thereafter, you will no longer be craving for it.

3. Spinning Facts. To make ethical manipulation successful, you need to think like a politician to yourself. Train your mind to spin facts. Make reason your own self and keep it under your control. Why do you think politicians win during elections? It is their capability to persuade the minds of the people. It is their ability to make voters see that they need their skills in Congress. To train your mind, you need to do exactly the same. Convince your mind that it needs to stop its bad habits or else something bad is going to happen. Persuade your mind to think about the positive things ahead once it puts a stop to the self-defeating urges and impulses that have been ingrained for many years.

4. Minimization of Impulses. The reason why people keep on behaving in accordance with their faulty lifestyle is the intensity of their feeling. When you start to minimize these impulses, it signals the mind that it is not as important as it used to be. It dissuades the mind of its need and significance in the body. Before, a person might think that he cannot quit smoking because he believes he's going to get sick. With the help of ethical manipulation, that person can control his mind and minimize the importance of this action. Soon enough, he starts to see he error of his ways and change for the better.

5. Diversion. Whenever the brain tells your body to act according to its impulses, create a diversion in a way that you expend your energy into something more productive. For example, if your mind shouts that you need a cigarette, do something that will get your mind off of that

urge. Play sports. Play the Computer. Start a conversation with your friends. Distract yourself until you no longer feel the need to do it.

6. Sarcasm. There are people who easily get hurt or offended when they are faced with critical confrontations. Sometimes people need a little bit of sarcasm so they can get the point without hurting for being offended. Psychiatrists use this method to people who are overly sensitive to words. Whenever they need to say something negative, they turn it into jokes that will make the client laugh but eventually understand the underlying meaning of the statements. If you lack assertiveness, and people keep taking you for granted because of it, you can use sarcasm to send them a message. In that way, you'll feel better about yourself. At the same time, you do not hurt anybody else.

7. Guilt Tripping. This is an effective method to stop yourself from giving in to your impulses. Whenever you feel like binge drinking or smoking, think about something that makes you feel guilty about it. If you have a son or a daughter, would you want them to experience the same fate as you? Remind yourself that secondhand smoking is more dangerous than first and smoking. Your family can still inhale fragments of substances from cigarettes hours after your last smoke. These substances are present in your clothes, your skin, and your breath. Merely talking to them can cause illnesses to your family. Are you willing to rest your safety because of your selfish needs?

8. Flattery. When you flatter yourself, that it doesn't necessarily mean that you are narcissistic. Sometimes, these simple things can uplift

your spirit and boost your determination. When you factor your mind after a good action, your mind secretes "feel-good" hormones. It makes your mind repeat the same good deed over and over again.

9. Isolation. This method does not mean to isolate yourself from the world. It is just that there are people who keep influencing you to employ your bad habits. Isolate yourself from those people. If you want to stop smoking, stay away from your friends who have the tendency to convince you to smoke again. If you want to lose weight, isolate yourself from unhealthy foods. If possible, get rid of any junk food and fatty foods from your food storage units and refrigerator. Exchange it all with healthy fruits and vegetables.

10. Brain Training. In order to rewire your brain, you need to get to know yourself and get acquainted with the reasons you have bad habits. There are people who engage in binge-drinking, binge-eating, and cigarette-smoking when they are stressed. Getting to the reason behind your impulses allows you to maintain a clear mindset even in you are anxious or pressured. Train your mind to do productive things during stressful situations. In that way, you can retain your mind to get rid of these ingrained habits.

Chapter 5

Mind Control

What is Mind Control?

The way that there are such a significant number of names demonstrates an absence of understanding which takes into consideration disarray and bending (particularly by those utilizing it secretly for their own advantage!!)

How about we concur that mind control goes under the umbrella of influence and impact - how to change individuals' convictions and practices.

Some will contend that everything is control. Be that as it may, in saying this, significant differentiations are lost. It's substantially more helpful to consider impact a continuum. Toward one side we have moral and conscious impacts that regard the individual and their privileges. At the opposite end we have dangerous impacts which strip the individual of their personality, freedom and capacity to think basically or intelligently.

It is at this end we find dangerous factions and organizations. These gatherings use duplicity and mind control strategies to exploit the shortcomings, just as the qualities, of the individuals, to fulfill the requirements and wants of the clique chiefs themselves.

A one-on-one clique is a private relationship where one individual maltreatment their capacity to control and endeavor the other, e.g., educator/understudy, advisor/customer, minister/admirer, spouse/husband. This cultic relationship is a variant of the bigger gatherings, and might be significantly progressively ruinous in light of the fact that constantly and consideration is coordinated towards only one person.

So what is mind control?

It's ideal to consider it an arrangement of impacts that altogether upsets a person at their very center, at the degree of their personality (their qualities, convictions, inclinations, choices, practices, connections and so forth.) making another pseudo-character or pseudopersonality.

It can obviously be utilized in useful ways, for instance with addicts, however here we are discussing circumstances that are naturally terrible or unscrupulous.

The analyst Philip Zimbardo says that mind control is a "procedure by which individual or aggregate opportunity of decision and activity is undermined by specialists or organizations that alter or contort recognition, inspiration, influence, comprehension or potentially social results" and he recommends that everybody is powerless to such control.

It isn't some old puzzle known to a chosen few, it is a mix of words and gathering weights, bundled so that it enables a controller to make reliance in their devotees, settling on their choices for them while enabling them to feel that they are autonomous and allowed to choose. The individual being mind controlled doesn't know about the impact procedure, nor of the progressions happening inside themselves.

There are some significant focuses that should be made entirely unmistakable.

Most importantly, it is an unpretentious and tricky procedure. Unpretentious, implying that the individual doesn't know about the degree of the impact being forced upon them. Along these lines they roll out little improvements after some time, accepting that they are settling on choices for themselves, when, actually, every one of the choices are being made for them. Treacherous in light of the fact that it's proposed to capture and do hurt.

What's more, it is a procedure, in that it doesn't occur in a moment. It requires some investment, in spite of the fact that the time span will rely upon such factors as the strategies utilized, the aptitude of the controller, the term of presentation to the methods and other social and individual elements. These days controllers are adequately gifted that it can happen in just a couple of hours.

There is power included. There could conceivably be physical power, yet there certainly is mental and social power and weight.

Mind control versus Brainwashing

Steve Hassan makes a fascinating qualification between mental control and indoctrinating. He says that in indoctrinating the unfortunate casualty realizes that the assailant is a foe. For instance, detainees of war realize that the individual doing the mentally programming or potentially torment is an adversary and frequently they comprehend that staying alive relies upon changing their conviction framework. They are constrained, regularly with physical power, into doing things they would not ordinarily do. Notwithstanding, when the unfortunate casualty escapes from the impact of the adversary, the impacts of the mentally programming every now and again vanish.

Mind control is progressively inconspicuous and advanced in light of the fact that the individual doing the controls is regularly viewed as a companion or an instructor, so the injured individual isn't really attempting to shield themselves. Truth be told, the person in question might be a 'willing' member, and, accepting that the controller has their eventual benefits as a primary concern, they regularly giving private data energetically, which is then utilized against them to proceed with the mind control.

This makes mind control as hazardous, if not more along these lines, than physical intimidation. As such, it tends to be much more powerful than torment, physical maltreatment, drugs and so on.

That merits rehashing. As a main priority control, there might be no physical pressure or viciousness, however it can really be significantly more powerful in controlling an individual.

That is on the grounds that compulsion can change conduct, however coercive influence (mind control) will change convictions, frames of mind, thinking procedures and conduct (essentially a character change). What's more, the 'person in question' cheerfully and effectively takes an interest in the changes, trusting it is best for them!

So later on, to acknowledge that somebody they trusted and loved has deluded and controlled them is exceptionally troublesome, and is one reason that it is difficult for individuals to perceive mind control. Notwithstanding when the unfortunate casualty is free of the impact of the manipulative character, the dispositions, convictions, and practices endure, in huge part in light of the fact that the injured individual accepts they have settled on these choices themselves (the impacts of choices we make ourselves are more grounded and more durable than choices we realize we have been pushed to make), and to some degree on the grounds that the individual wouldn't like to concede that they have been controlled without their knowing, they would prefer not to accept that they have been deceived by a 'companion'.

You can peruse progressively about how every one of the progressions are achieved utilizing mind control in these articles on narcissistic beaus and narcissistic spouses.

A gun to the head

Controllers are attached to stating that nobody is holding a gun to the controlled individual's head, and this is incredible in two different ways. To the pariah who doesn't comprehend mind control, it is hard to contend with.

For the controlled individual, they realize this is valid. Nobody has really held a weapon to their head, so it strengthens the possibility that they have chosen for themselves. Also, choices we have made ourselves are significantly more dominant and the impacts last more, so it further moves the controlled individual more profound into the truth made by the mind control.

Who uses Mind Control?

Who might utilize these methods, obliterating the lives of others for their own narrow minded advantages? Or then again controlling others just on the grounds that they can or on the grounds that they need the control? The appropriate response is insane people, or sociopaths, and narcissists. Most likely by far most of extraordinary manipulative people who use mind control fit the profile of an insane person or a narcissist. What's more, the explanation they can do it is on the grounds that they have no heart!

Since individuals don't have the foggiest idea what precisely an insane person or a narcissist is, the controller is regularly called something different, an oppressive spouse or a controlling wife or controlling husband, a desirous sweetheart, a verbally injurious man or a severe chief. Closer assessment frequently uncovers these individuals to have a character issue.

Each individual is vulnerable. That includes you!

It is a fantasy that solitary feeble and powerless individuals are vulnerable, or that there is some kind of problem with them. Actually, the conviction that "it could never transpire" makes an individual especially vulnerable to mind control apparatuses, on the grounds that they're not watchful for them!

The most ideal approach to shield yourself from being enlisted by a faction (it is a fantasy that individuals join cliques, they are really selected) and being exposed to mind control is to see how a religion capacities just as the clique strategies that are utilized to draw in and keep individuals.

For instance, Robert Cialdini has depicted six standards of impact that he portrays as weapons of impact. It appears that these capacity in all social orders on the planet, and they are really helpful as far as enabling society to stay stable and flourish. He discusses correspondence, duty and consistency, social verification, affability, authority and shortage. He calls them weapons of impact since they work outside of the consciousness of a great many people and thus factions exploit them to control and impact their individuals.

What Affects the Effectiveness of Mind Control

- The damaging impacts of mind control are relative to:
- The procedures utilized
- The quantity of procedures
- Regardless of whether there is trance and additionally trancelike personality control utilized,
- How regularly the individual is presented to it and for to what extent
- That they are so near the religion head, what amount direct contact there is
- The ability of the controller
- How much introduction to the outside world is permitted
- Nearness of sexual maltreatment
- Regardless of whether the part keeps on having support from family and companions.

For instance, an individual who has lived and worked in a religion domain for a long time where the individuals live respectively, who once in a while leaves the gathering compound and who has visit, direct contact with the faction chief will have experienced considerably more the impacts of clique control than somebody who goes to a 2 hour class given by the clique head once per week for 2 months.

In one-on-one cliques, in a close association with a sociopath, for instance, a couple circumstance, where all the consideration is given to one injured individual, the outcomes can be aggravating. Complex injury is the term being utilized these days to portray what befalls kids who are raised by psychopathic or narcissistic guardians.

Techniques Used in Mind Control

Present day mind control is both innovative and mental. Tests demonstrate that basically by uncovering the techniques for mind control, the impacts can be diminished or disposed of, at any rate for mind control publicizing and promulgation. Increasingly hard to counter are the physical interruptions, which the military-mechanical complex keeps on creating and enhance.

1. **Education** — This is the most self-evident, yet still remains the most treacherous. It has consistently been an eventual tyrant's definitive dream to "teach" normally receptive youngsters, subsequently it has been a focal segment to Communist and Fascist oppressive regimes from the beginning of time. Nobody has been increasingly instrumental in uncovering the motivation of present day instruction than Charlotte Iserbyt — one can start investigation into this region by downloading a free PDF of her book, The Deliberate Dumbing Down of America, which reveals the job of Globalist establishments in forming a future planned to deliver servile automatons reigned over by a completely taught, mindful exclusive class.

2. **Promotions and Propaganda** – Edward Bernays has been referred to as the creator of the consumerist culture that was planned principally to focus on individuals' mental self portrait

(or scarcity in that department) so as to transform a need into a need. This was at first imagined for items, for example, cigarettes, for instance. Nonetheless, Bernays additionally noted in his 1928 book, Propaganda, that "purposeful publicity is the official arm of the imperceptible government." This can be seen most unmistakably in the advanced police state and the developing native nark culture, enveloped with the pseudo-enthusiastic War on Terror. The expanding union of media has empowered the whole corporate structure to converge with government, which currently uses the idea of promulgation arrangement. Media; print, motion pictures, TV, and link news would now be able to work flawlessly to incorporate a general message which appears to have the ring of truth since it originates from such a significant number of sources, at the same time. When one moves toward becoming sensitive to recognizing the fundamental "message," one will see this engraving all over. What's more, this isn't even to specify subliminal informing.

3. **Prescient Programming** – Many still deny that prescient writing computer programs is genuine. Prescient programming has its causes in predominately elitist Hollywood, where the big screen can offer a major vision of where society is going. Simply glance back at the books and motion pictures which you thought were implausible, or "sci-fi" and investigate society today. For a nitty gritty breakdown of explicit models, Vigilant Citizen is an

incredible asset that will most likely make you take a gander at "amusement" in a totally unique light.

4. **Sports, Politics, Religion** – Some may resent seeing religion, or even legislative issues, put together with sports as a technique for mind control. The focal topic is the equivalent all through: isolate and prevail. The systems are very straightforward: impede common propensity of individuals to participate for their endurance, and train them to frame groups bowed on control and winning. Sports has consistently had a job as a key diversion that corrals innate propensities into a non-significant occasion, which in present day America has arrived at silly extents where challenges will break out over a game VIP leaving their city, yet basic human issues, for example, freedom are chuckled away as immaterial.

5. **Food, Water, and Air** – Additives, poisons, and other nourishment harms actually modify mind science to make mildness and indifference. Fluoride in drinking water has been demonstrated to bring down IQ; Aspartame and MSG are excitotoxins which energize synapses until they kick the bucket; and simple access to the inexpensive food that contains these toxins by and large has made a populace that needs center and inspiration for a functioning way of life. The vast majority of the cutting edge world is flawlessly prepped for uninvolved responsiveness — and acknowledgment — of the authoritarian tip top.

6. **Medications** — This can be any addictive substance, however the mission of mind controllers is to be certain you are dependent on something. One noteworthy arm of the cutting edge mind control motivation is psychiatry, which expects to characterize all individuals by their issue, instead of their human potential. This was foreshadowed in books, for example, Brave New World. Today, it has been taken to considerably assist limits as a medicinal oppression has grabbed hold where about everybody has a type of confusion — especially the individuals who question authority. The utilization of nerve tranquilizes in the military has prompted record quantities of suicides. To top it all off, the cutting edge medication state currently has over 25% of U.S. youngsters on mind-desensitizing drugs.

7. **Military testing** — The military has a long history as the proving ground for mind control. The military personality is maybe the most pliable, as the individuals who seek after life in the military by and large resound to the structures of progression, control, and the requirement for unchallenged submission to a mission. For the expanding number of military individual scrutinizing their influence, an ongoing story featured DARPA's arrangements for transcranial mind control head protectors that will keep them centered.

8. **Electromagnetic range** — An electromagnetic soup encompasses all of us, charged by present day gadgets of comfort which have been appeared to directly affect mind work. In an

implicit affirmation of what is conceivable, one scientist has been working with a "divine being head protector" to instigate dreams by adjusting the electromagnetic field of the mind. Our advanced soup has us latently washed by conceivably mind-changing waves, while a wide scope of potential outcomes, for example, phone towers is currently accessible to the eventual personality controller for more straightforward mediation.

Mind control is more common than most people think. It is not easy to detect because of its subtle nature. In many instances, it happens under what is perceived as normal circumstances like through education, religion, TV programs, advertisements and so much more. Cults and their leadership use mind control to influence their members and control whatever they do. It is not easy to detect mind control. However, when one realizes it, they can get out and start afresh.

Uses of Mind Control Techniques

Individuals that use mind control techniques to manipulate or persuade others do so with various goals in site. In this chapter, we discuss the uses of these techniques in relation to the victims of mind control and what the perpetrators wish to achieve.

Isolation

Physical segregation can be ground-breaking, yet notwithstanding when physical disengagement is unimaginable or not pragmatic, controllers will commonly endeavor to detach you rationally. This might be accomplished in various ways from multi week courses in the nation to scrutinizing your family and friend network. Restricting some other impact by controlling data stream is a definitive objective.

Criticism

Analysis might be utilized as a disconnection device. The controllers will more often than not talk in "us against them" terms, reprimand the outside world and guarantee their very own prevalence. As indicated by them, you should feel fortunate to be related with them.

Peer Pressure and social proof

The individuals who endeavor to control enormous gatherings of individuals will normally utilize social evidence and friend strain to mentally program newcomers. Social confirmation is a mental marvel where (a few) individuals expect that the activities and convictions of others are fitting and, in light of the fact that "everybody does that", must be legitimized. This works particularly well when an individual isn't sure what to think, how to carry on, or what to do. Many individuals in such circumstances will just take a gander at what others do and do likewise.

Fear of alienation

Newcomers to manipulative gatherings will for the most part get a warm welcome and will shape various new kinships that appear to be a lot further and more significant than anything they have ever experienced. Later on, if any questions emerge, these connections will turn into an amazing asset to hold them in the gathering. Regardless of whether they aren't totally persuaded, the life in the outside world may appear to be forlorn.

Reiteration

Consistent redundancy is another amazing influence device. In spite of the fact that it might appear to be too shortsighted to be in any way successful, yet rehashing same message again and again makes it commonplace and simpler to recollect. At the point when reiteration is joined with social evidence, it conveys the message without a fall flat.

Fatigue

Exhaustion and lack of sleep bring about physical and mental tiredness. When you are physically drained and less alert, you are increasingly defenseless to influence. An investigation referenced in the Journal of Experimental Psychology demonstrates that people who had not rested for just 21 hours were increasingly vulnerable to proposal.

Forming a New Identity

At last, controllers need to re-characterize your personality. They need you to quit acting naturally and become a robot, somebody who carelessly pursues their requests. Utilizing all strategies and mind control methods referenced above, they will endeavor to separate an admission from you — some type of affirmation that you accept that they are great individuals doing something worth being thankful for (slight varieties are conceivable). In the first place it may be something apparently inconsequential like concurring that the individuals from the gathering are fun and adoring individuals or that a portion of their perspectives are in reality substantial. When you acknowledge that one seemingly insignificant detail, you might be increasingly prepared to acknowledge another and afterward another and another… Before you know it, out of want to be steady with what you do and say, you start distinguishing as one of the gatherings. This is especially amazing in the event that you realize that your admissions were recorded or taped — just in the event that you overlook, there is a physical confirmation of your new personality.

Presently in the wake of perusing this, you might ponder about "gatherings" throughout your life. Is it accurate to say that they are controlling you?

How about we imagine you joined Greenpeace. Everything began with a little gift, at that point some kind of fun occasion (loads of new companions), and, before you know it, you are sitting in a little vessel dissenting Shell's penetrating in the polar area while your training and vocation are put on hold. What occurred here? Did Greenpeace control you into doing this? No. They impacted you. While they got you to accomplish something you could never consider doing, Greenpeace doesn't utilize you to further their own potential benefit. They requested that you do what they accept is correct (despite the fact that sentiments may change) and you concurred — there is no close to home addition here.

Contrast that with, suppose, a controlling karate instructor who is verbally and physically injurious toward his understudies while anticipating absolute deference and compliance consequently, who makes them think like they are the main gathering of individuals who are going to realize some extraordinary mystery that will put both Terminator and Rambo to disgrace. Regardless of whether his intentions here are monetary or a basic want to control and feel predominant, there is no uncertainty he is utilizing mind control methods referenced previously.

Presence of certifications (as personal growth system) is another evidence that reiteration works. On the off chance that you can influence yourself through redundancy, odds are somebody may endeavor to utilize reiteration to control you into deduction and carrying on with a specific goal in mind.

How Effective are Mind Control Techniques?

Techniques in mind control are very effective in achieving what they have been set out to. The strategies which control others brain is an entrancing type of ruinous power that still exists in the public arena. The psyche is increasingly responsive in seeing the exercises of outside world.

Our brain retains each data and channels the required one. Our cognizant and subliminal personality channels this information. These snippets of data are generally prepared by the mind. Out of 1000s of data that we see through our five faculties just a couple of them are we intentionally mindful of.

What's more, this sifting relies on specific conditions. In this way, this made it progressively helpless against such controls where NLP is an integral asset to control an individual's musings.

The mind control strategies can impact one's procedure activities on the grounds that these measures are the aftereffect of the contemplations in your brain at first controlled. Such techniques depend on the Neuro-Linguistic Programming (NLP) that is fit for controlling individuals' psyche with the well-prepared methodologies and examples.

Thus, it is conceivable to trick one's brain by putting an item or anything in the region of the subject that sidesteps the cognizant personality which is picked by the intuitive personality.

Hardly any stunts of the mentalist work in this standard as they may wear a red tie that will be overlooked by the cognizant personality as though irrelevant, and encouraged into the subliminal personality of the eyewitness unwittingly utilizing certain systems. Presumably, it is finished utilizing the word 'READ' in the discussion or some different methods which will trigger the shading 'RED' in the onlooker's psyche.

These musings get prompted in the spectator in precise habits that are utilized by exceptionally gifted NLP experts. The truth of the matter is that increasingly unobtrusive the recommendations, more the intuitive personality get impacted.

Mind Control and Decision Making

Cult individuals and individuals in damaging connections normally accept that they have settled on their own choices and are proceeding to do as such - notwithstanding when to pariahs their convictions and their rationale appear to be abnormal and practically unbelievable! Be that as it may, their volition, their choice, has been seriously constrained. Religion individuals have been persuaded a wide range of things, that they are a piece of a tip top gathering, that they have uncommon or significant data that can change or spare the world, their pioneer is perfect, their families are awful/malicious/keeping them down, that they will be unable to make due outside the gathering, in addition to other things.

On the off chance that you have a relative or a companion in a religion, you will perceive a portion of these things!

Keep in mind that mind control (once in a while alluded to as coercive control) is a procedure and that religion individuals have arrived at where they are slowly and carefully. Their existence has been moved as a result of their participation of the gathering, and inside this reality they accept they are settling on their own choices, despite the fact that these choices are frequently intended to keep them caught in the gathering.

Notwithstanding when they are given logical inconsistencies, irrationality and incongruence's in what they state and do, they will frequently contend to keep up their conviction frameworks unblemished, for the very reason that they accept that they have picked and have settled on their own choices about it. Also, to be sure, in their new, forced reality, all the time there are no inconsistencies or incongruence's for them! (Keep in mind their basic reasoning capacities have been stifled).

Individuals likewise create convictions to enable them to manage their mind control circumstance. These convictions can really hamper recuperation later on, as clarified in this article about harsh moms.

Manipulations and Mind Control

Mental manipulation is a kind of social impact that expects to change the conduct or impression of others through roundabout, misleading, or wicked tactics. By propelling the interests of the manipulator, regularly to another's detriment, such strategies could be viewed as exploitative and insidious.

Social impact isn't really negative. For instance, individuals, companions, family and specialists, can attempt to induce to change unmistakably unhelpful propensities and practices. Social impact is commonly seen to be innocuous when it regards the privilege of the affected to acknowledge or dismiss it, and isn't unduly coercive. Contingent upon the specific circumstance and inspirations, social impact may establish insidious control.

One may not realize they are being manipulated. Below we discuss a few examples of manipulative situations for your understanding.

Examples of Manipulative Behaviors

1. Minimizing

    Manipulative conduct includes limiting its consequences for other people. At the point when the beneficiary of a frightful or harsh remark makes some noise, the manipulative individual, rather than being worried that they have disturbed somebody, will counter with the answer, "I was just kidding. Wouldn't you be able to take a joke?" or "You are SO touchy!". This totally limits the passionate effect and leaves the beneficiary with nowhere to go. They are left feeling they are to be faulted.

    Another model, "I am feeling so focused on today" (seeking after compassion and backing). Controllers reaction: "You don't have the foggiest idea what stress is!". In the event that you get furious, you will perpetually be told "I was just kidding!". There is no approval, sympathy or backing. Controllers can likewise be dug in narcissists.

2. Never Accepting Fault

    Manipulative individuals accuse every other person, they once in a while acknowledge their part to play in life circumstances. Their conduct is frequently observed by the as a reaction to something another person has done. On the off chance that they hadn't irritated me, it could never have occurred. On the off chance that they had tuned in, I would need to act along these lines and so on. They like to exonerate themselves from any moral duty regarding their activities. A genuine model: you stumble over their shoes/sack and so forth in the night as they have set them too close to the entryway. When you fall over them you are accused by the controller since you should watch where you are going or you ought to have turned on the light (the way that they left their effects where individuals walk isn't considered or referenced).

3. Non-verbal manipulation

Eye rolling, moaning, head shaking – these are a portion of the run of the mill practices displayed by a controller. They show dissatisfaction or frustration without saying a word and leave the unfortunate casualty feeling disgrace and blame. It is all piece of the way toward making someone else question themselves – a moderate dribble disintegration of their certainty happens after some time.

4. Gaslighting

This manipulative conduct can without much of a stretch make an individual vibe they are going insane. Gaslighting includes planting false data as valid so as to make someone else question themselves and their discernments. This is shrewdly done over a moderate period and can leave an individual befuddled and uncertain of themselves. Your accomplice may swear they informed you concerning the gathering on the end of the week and, despite the fact that they didn't as a general rule, the additional time goes on, the less certainty you have in your rendition. There should be a conscious, deceptive perspective to it — as it were, there should lie.

Here are indications of gaslighting:

- You are continually re-thinking yourself

- You ask yourself, "Am I excessively touchy?" twelve times each day.

- You regularly feel befuddled and even insane.

- You can't get why, with such a significant number of clearly beneficial things throughout your life, you aren't more joyful.

- You realize something is horrendously off-base, however you can never entirely express what it is, even to yourself.

- You start deceiving maintain a strategic distance from the put downs   and reality turns.

- You experience difficulty settling on straightforward choices.

- You have the feeling that you used to be an altogether different individual – progressively sure, increasingly carefree, progressively loose.

- You feel miserable and sad.

- You feel as if you can't do anything right.

- You wonder in the event that you are a "sufficient" sweetheart/spouse/worker/companion; little girl.

5. Disregarding your Efforts

Off camera, your manipulative accomplice may discover unpretentious approaches to obstruct and disappoint you. This mystery, and the resulting disappointment for you, enables them to feel in charge in a detached forceful way. For instance – they 'overlook' to inform you regarding a significant telephone message and therefore you miss a significant gathering. When they realize something is imperative to you, they will embrace unobtrusive conduct that incites an enthusiastic reaction from you. One of the manners in which they control and manipulative is by knowing your shortcomings and squeezing those enthusiastic catches. For instance – I dated a man who might be severe with my canine and yell at my pooch, realizing that it would disturb me. The pooch turned into an authentic objective for inspiring feeling in me and in this manner enabling him to feel in charge. When I responded, it would 'clearly' bring about fault being set upon me and how excessively touchy I am.

On the off chance that you are in a race to get some place, a manipulative individual may drag their heels and defer you much further. Everything is done so unobtrusively that it is difficult to point to explicit proof and at last the normal individual starts to unwind while the controller feels all the more dominant. Retaining data is a typical strategy, controllers revel in the way that they have data and that you are unaware.

6. Being told that You Don't Listen

A haughty strategy that places the controller in the 'equitable' position and accept that the audience isn't seeing effectively. A rational adjusted individual will likewise take a gander at their own relational abilities as opposed to reprimanding another for not listening accurately. This serves to keep you decreased and undermine your certainty. It keeps the controller in the 'control situate'.

7. Leading Statements

"Wouldn't you say that... "

"Why have you done it that way?"

Suggestions to Decide Independently Without Manipulations

If you want to be able to think more independently and improve your decision making skills, following the below suggestions will help you a great deal:

Think Flexibly

As intricacy expands, consistency unavoidably decreases, and thusly, vulnerability and vagueness will likewise ascend simultaneously.

Most basic leadership draws near, be that as it may, depend on objective reasoning and depend on memory and rationale - the progressing effect of the logical transformation of the sixteenth century. Such procedures will in general have an understood presumption: that the past gives a helpful and dependable reason for anticipating what's to come.

Get Creative

At whatever point we face an issue and it feels just as the circumstance is sad, or that there are no more alternatives accessible to us, it might quit feeling like a basic leadership challenge by any stretch of the imagination.

Be that as it may, it is. The issue is just that, in such conditions, the old critical thinking approach, in view of past understanding, is bombing us, since that experience clearly isn't giving a reasonable course. What is required here is a profoundly unique type of basic leadership: one dependent on innovativeness.

Step Outside Your Comfort Zone

Applying an imaginative methodology will regularly take boldness. We as a whole will in general have a characteristic dread of deserting the commonplace and moving toward our difficulties in new ways. In any case, when we stick to the known, we aren't probably going to do much learning. To push ahead, we should escape our customary range of familiarity and venture into vagueness. There is actually no other method to figure out how to deal with the advancing difficulties of the cutting edge world. When you face such circumstances, attempt to advise yourself that if things around you are changing while you stay in your customary range of familiarity, at that point in viable terms, you are going in reverse. That implies you will in all likelihood have an issue coming.

Let Solutions Emerge

Another issue made by the vulnerability around what the future may resemble is that it is regularly important to begin moving advances before the last goal is in sight.

In the old 'critical thinking' world, it was regularly conceivable to work through an issue to find to the solution, at that point essentially set about actualizing that arrangement. Today, this kind of methodology would be similar to endeavoring to hang tight for all the traffic lights on your course to turn green before venturing out from home.

Feeling 'Right' is No Guide

We as a whole utilize various oblivious mental inclinations and easy routes, even in the most fundamental everyday exercises. Without them, our cognizant personality would be overwhelmed by the quantity of routine choices required for living.

Notwithstanding, shockingly, such inclinations bring about predispositions that can, and as often as possible do, prompt blunders. To exacerbate this issue, we get no psychological cautioning chimes when this occurs - when we are incorrect, it feels precisely equivalent to when we are correct.

Realize that Objectivity is a Myth

A major piece of the motivation behind why it is so natural to accept that we are correct is that it is normal to expect that our cognizant experience of the world is "exact", and that we have a decent handle of what's going on around us. In any case, mental research exhibits that we really have a solid inclination for being correct, and that our psyches can persuade us that we "know", notwithstanding when we are mixed up.

Welcome Alternative Perspectives

A basic methodology that defeats the mistake inclined subjectivity of our believing is to figure out how to invite elective points of view. We should ace effectively looking for proof that goes against what we right now accept, and perhaps the most straightforward methods for doing so is to take a functioning enthusiasm for assessments that contrast from our own.

Seek to Disprove Your Own Ideas

There is one answer for our absence of objectivity and propensity to accept that we are correct that is amazing to such an extent that it lies at the core of logical reasoning. In science, speculations are perceived for what they are: working standards to be utilized until disproven, so, all things considered they become supplanted with more up to date and increasingly helpful hypotheses.

Individuals that use mind control techniques do so to gain control over their victims. The mind control techniques they use are very effective in giving them what they want. Victims of mind control are unable to make independent decisions, yet they think they do. It is important to identify manipulation and take back control to make your own decisions. Following the suggestions in this chapter, you can now be able to make independent decisions that bring you joy.

Chapter 6

Maximize Your Potential

When you are into your goal-setting season, it is important to understand that when you are setting your goals, be sure to give yourself the best opportunity there is for success. This is important because when you look at the failure rates recorded by Forbes, they show that 92 percent of people fail to hit their targets. This is an indication that it is sometimes easy to fail than succeed. We shall also give you a four-week action plan to guide you on becoming the kind of person you want to be.

1. Aim higher, but start low as you celebrate your achievements and keep going

Most people find it fun setting big and bold goals. While it is true that huge goals are exciting and inspiring and can also help you in not only achieving but also exceeding your full potential, setting big goals can sometimes be daunting in the first few days. A perfect way to counter that is by breaking your huge goals down into a series of small achievable goals.

For instance, if you are a marathoner and you are just starting out, your first goal might be to run for just fifteen to twenty minutes per run during the first week and then gradually increase your time by, say, five minutes per week for the next two months. Taking this approach will allow you to have some early success that will allow you to build momentum and increase your confidence. You'll feel encouraged to raise the weekly goal by ten minutes in the next two months and later fifteen minutes per week during the last two months.

When you take these small steps and increase them by small amounts, you will be put in a good position after some time. In the long run, this will help you achieve your huge bold goal. When it comes to setting your huge goal, the more you are able to divide that elephant, the higher the chances you will have in achieving your goal.

2. Don't let rely on others to set your goals

Letting other people set or modify goals for you can bring several damaging effects and can prevent you from achieving those goals. The reason is that they will be no longer be your goals, and you will not have a sense of ownership or even commitment, because it is someone else's goal. Additionally, when other people set a goal for you, they can see you being more aggressive than you are and hence set goals that are higher than what you believe you can do. Lack of belief can lead to quitting when you experience the first challenge. If you need to involve people, have your set goal, and then they can help you in achieving it well, but do not let them set a new goal for you.

3. Have a clear mental view of what success looks like

Having smart goals will help you have clarity and a reasonable deadline to achieve your goals. Small goals consist of the following:

- *Specific.* Your goal must be defined clearly. Instead of saying that you need more money in a month, you must be specific on the amount of money you want—for example, $20,000 or $100,000 per month.

- *Measurable.* You need to have a certain measure that will allow you to know that you have actually achieved your goal.

- *Attainable.* Although it seems fine to set goals that make you stretch and feel challenged, you must not set goals that are impossible, because it will only lead to frustrations.

It is hard to achieve something whose appearance you don't know. Therefore, for you to achieve success in your goals, you must have a clear image of what success looks like. The secret is to have a clear goal so that you can put in place a clear plan in achieving it.

I had a client who was looking ahead to increase his revenue by between 50 and 100 percent in the following year. They were happy that they had a huge goal. However, the challenge was that the plan to have a 50 percent increase was not the same as when increasing it by 100 percent. Therefore, you must know exactly what plans are going to be implemented. You cannot implement an old plan and just hope, because hope is not a strategy. Having clear goals will help you come up with clear plans, which will increase your chances of achieving success.

4. Know why your goals are important

If you don't understand why your goals are important to you, it will hard to put in the necessary effort. Understanding the reason why your goals are essential will you give a strong sense of purpose, which will keep you motivated when going through difficult moments. When you don't have a sense of purpose, when things do not go as expected, there is nothing that will stop you from downgrading your target.

For you to achieve your huge goals, you must remain firm on your goal, but be flexible on your approach. Having a strong reason for achieving your goal will help your eyes remain focused on the final prize and motivate you to keep fighting even during tough moments.

5. Keep track of your performance

I strongly believe in the saying "What gets measured gets done." But I strongly believe more in the power of motivation. When you divide the elephant into small goals, when you begin to achieve them, it will increase both the belief in your approach and the confidence that success is achievable.

If you are working as a team, be sure to share the progress to your team when you track the performance. Usually, people will like to know the progress, especially when the going gets tougher. Sometimes when your head is down and you are gearing toward the finishing line and you don't know just how close you are, hearing the progress will encourage you to make the final stretch and get over the line.

6. Look for knowledge and not results

Keeping your focus on the excitement that comes from discovering, exploring, improving, and experimenting will always fuel your motivation. When you concentrate mainly on results, your motivation will die anytime you hit a storm. Therefore, you must put your key focus on the journey and not on your destination. Keep track of what you are experiencing on the way and look for areas that you can improve.

7. Don't allow yourself to stagnate

When you feel as though you are not learning new ideas in either your personal or professional life, it may be the best time to change. For you to grow, you must avoid stagnation at all costs. Through this, you will be able to face new challenges and overcome any obstacles on your way.

8. Create a positive working environment

There is no doubt that people will perform as good as their working environment. Having a poor working environment can lead to unengaged and unproductive staff, and their negative attitude to work will be reflected in the type of products and services provided. If you want to succeed in what you are doing, you should learn how to create a positive working environment. Below are the tips for creating a positive working environment:

- *Practice safety in the workplace.* No one will want to work in an environment that is not safe. If they do, they will be prone to injuries. You are legally obliged to adhere to both health and safety regulations so that you can have a safe working environment. If you or even your employee experience uneasiness while working, it will be hard to work to your full potential.

- *Embrace a positive reinforcement and be friendly.* Practicing saying kind words can go a long way in business. How you engage with people can lead to failure or success in your chosen sector. You must understand that there are some duties you cannot accomplish alone without your employees, and that is why you need to acknowledge them as much as possible. When you have a practice of reinforcing your employees positively, you will boost their satisfaction and engagement, and they will be happy to know that they are making an impact on your business. So be sure to say a kind word to them so that they can feel valued. Workers are likely to put more effort when working for an employer who is approachable. For this reason, it is wise to learn people's names, put a smile on your face, and say hi to your members in the morning before starting the day's work.

- *Have a habit of celebrating success.* It is good when starting a meeting that you begin with positive things not just concerning your business but also concerning those who have made that possible. Single out an individual or a department for a job well done. Have a note of whom you have recently thanked, and also look for ways to recognize members of your staff who might feel undervalued in their duties.

- *Encourage fun in the workplace.* An office full of events will lead to a lack of creativity, motivation, and satisfaction in the job. Always provide the right balance between work and play in the office to allow people to chat and have fun. For instance, you should give your staff a fun breakout, and you can also introduce casual Fridays or even themed days, where people can come dressed casually.

- *Practice random acts of kindness.* All of us love something given for free. Show your staff how you value them through the provision of random gifts. For instance, you can decide to offer pizzas for every member of your staff or bring snacks or even a bottle of beer or wine at the end of the working week. This will make people wish the weekend will end faster so that they can report to their duties on Monday.

Four-week action plan to become the person you want to be

Before you call yourself a professional of any sector, you must have gone through the whole process of training to learn the operations of that industry in and out. One place that people lose the point is in thinking that they are professionals just because they are doing something pertaining to an industry. They forget that they don't actually know how to do it. That is not a sign of professionalism but a sign of delusion.

Even if you think you are brilliant, if you do not have the ability to bring out your expertise effortlessly, the world will never experience that brilliance.

However, there is hope, because you can learn to become anything you want to be. If you have identified what you want to be and you don't know how to start, I shall help you with my four-week plan. I have prepared an easy-to-follow plan for four weeks, which will help you become the kind of person you want to be confidently.

If you follow this plan, in four weeks, you will have done what you have so much desired in a professional way. You will also have a sure method on how to produce infinite results effortlessly the professional way.

Week 1: Learn to practice

When starting in any profession, the first thing that you need to know is to get into the habit of working in that specific industry. Allow me to say something that many young professions will not like: most of your work as a beginner sucks. Most professions who are just starting out are arrogant and think that they know it all. These are people who have just started, and their work is terrible and worthless.

What they are not aware of is that, not only will they fail to make a good name for themselves, but they are doing harm to themselves by giving their client such a bad impression concerning their work. They value quantity instead of quality. There is an important thing that should, however, be noted. It is not only the bad professional that produces bad results; goods professionals also give bad results many times. The only different thing between bad and good professionals is that good people don't allow anyone to see their bad stuff. Good professionals have one quality that bad people do not have, which is perspective.

Good people practice the habit of stepping out on their own and looking objectively at their work. They are aware that they cannot let their pride take over their work. If their work is bad, they are aware that it requires correction or should be trashed and cannot be forwarded as it is.

In the first week, the goal is to open up your creative thought process or the subconscious mind and then learn how to apply those thoughts into action.

Week 2: Build a framework

Thank you for joining us to week 2. You should, however, note that this is a continuation of what you learned in week 1, and so you should continue practicing what you learned in week 1. This means that by the time you reach week 4, you should be practicing what you've learned from week 1 to 3.

By now you must possess a generally good idea on how to capture your thoughts as they come. Your creativity should also be increasing. In week 2, the aim is to start gathering ideas and learning how to put them together.

At this point, your work is jumbled and all over the place. You are literally coming up with what is in your mind and have no thought process behind anything. You are just doing it for the sake of doing it.

In this week, you will do something different, which involves keeping a personal journal of what happened to you during the day concerning your project. Usually, it is done at night for the purpose of rewinding your day's events. Each day requires writing detailed information concerning your day from the time you woke up in the morning.

Ensure you have an outline that will act as a framework for your work in the future. Most half-baked professionals will produce a half-baked and scattered piece of work. When you have an outline on what you want to be, you will be able to easily collect your ideas and make them appear at the appropriate time and place. It is just like when in construction. The first thing is to lay the foundation before you start the construction. Without a firm foundation, your house will not be strong.

Again when we move into our new house, we will meet empty walls and also floors. It is from there that we will begin to move furniture and put up also decorations. It could be a foolish act to bring furniture in before building the house.

Week 3: Do your assignment

At week 3, we have a solid foundation to work on whatever our project may be. This is the point where you go ahead and implement what you have been having in your mind. In the past week, we have been throwing around many ideas. Our daily journals are basically ideas waiting to be implemented. At this time, you should have plenty of ideas about what you want to do.

And unlike the past two weeks, you are more flexible in the doing process. This means that you can go proceed to do what you want to do. The most important thing is to keep practicing what you have learned. Use these seven days to work on your project. Whether it's one piece per day or per week, this is not important. Only make sure you are doing it every day.

Week 4: Relook at your project and finalize

Looking at your project before making the final submission is important. This will help you remove mistakes that you might have made in your earlier work. In any kind of profession, you must take the time to relook at your work. This will not only save your image but will also ensure that you provide the best services to the world.

At this stage, you must keep learning more so that you can improve and not forget to apply what you have learned in your early stages. Make your dream career a reality, and give it as much time as possible for good results.

It's my hope that when you follow the above four-week plan, you will emerge being the kind of person you want to be. It all starts with decision-making and then dedicating yourself toward achieving your goal. There's nothing that can be achieved unless it is conquered in our minds, and so guiding our minds should be a priority in achieving our goals.

Chapter 7

Fundamental Concepts And Connection To Stoicism

J ust about every philosophy offers freedom of one form or another. Many focus on being free from hardship and suffering, whereas others offer freedom from ignorance, hopelessness and even oblivion. Stoicism offers several freedoms of its own, including freedom from passion, freedom from suffering and even freedom from chaos. However, one element of Stoic freedom that sets it apart from many other variations is the idea of being free from the inside out. While most traditions focus on being free from external factors, Stoicism focuses on being free from internal factors. These internal factors include passions, unbridled desire, and inner conflict. However, all of these combine to create the ultimate freedom—freedom of the mind. In short, as a person practices Stoicism they undergo a process that serves to free their mind of all the restrictions, delusions and sufferings that plague the average person.

Freeing the Mind from External Influences

At first glance freeing the mind may seem like a process that has little to do with the outside world. However, the fact is that many of the obstacles, restrictions and pitfalls that are found in a person's mind are put there by external forces. This can take extreme forms such as brainwashing, mental programming and the like, or it can take more subtle forms such as social values, religious belief systems and even advertising campaigns. In the end, the mind is constantly bombarded with information of various forms from outside influences. Even if the individual filters this information it still has a way of finding its way in, causing all sorts of internal conflict, doubt and confusion. This is where Stoicism can come to the rescue.

One way that Stoicism frees the mind from outside influences is that if places a strong focus on logic and wisdom. These attributes help the individual to keep from falling prey to the emotional manipulation that underscores much of modern media. Everything from the news to political campaigns and even advertising campaigns is designed to focus on a person's emotional triggers. By hitting the right nerve these outlets can influence people to buy products, vote for a particular candidate, or do any number of things without giving a second thought. However, the Stoic practitioner will apply logic and wisdom to the things they see and hear, determining their inherent veracity. More often than not the result is that the Stoic sees through the deception and is therefore able to avoid from making a decision they will later regret. This frees the mind from the hype and propaganda that saturates just about every strata of our society in this modern time.

Stoicism also places a high significance on ethics. The difference between Stoic ethics and conventional ethics is that Stoic ethics are based on the individual, not on the collective. This means that every Stoic has to decide what is ethical to them, not simply accept a preset list of dos and don'ts. While it may seem counter intuitive to reject social norms of behavior in order to achieve an ethical standard of behavior, the truth is that ethics must come from the inside out, not from the outside in. Zeno and his contemporaries believed that nature is just and correct, therefore each individual possesses an inherent sense of right and wrong. By following this internal moral compass the Stoic will free themselves from the social, religious and political influences that would try to persuade a person to follow their prescribed set of rules. Seeing as how these rules are usually designed to control human behavior, such a moral compass would go a long way to preserving the freedom of the individual's mind and soul.

Freeing the Mind from Internal Influences

As challenging as freeing oneself from external influences is, it is nothing compared to breaking free from internal influences. Emotions, desires, ambitions and other such inner drives can be the hardest things to be free of. After all, you can run away from just about anyone or anything, but you can never run away from yourself. Wherever you go, you will always find yourself there. Fortunately, Zeno and his contemporaries realized that true freedom and liberation from suffering had to be achieved from the inside out. Therefore, he set about establishing the

Stoic principles in order to help the average person achieve this goal. The end result is that as a person follows the Stoic tradition they will become free from internal influences as well as external ones.

No internal influence is as strong as a person's emotions. A person's emotional reaction to a situation serves to interpret that situation in a biased and often inaccurate way. Fear can make any situation seem far worse than it actually is, and anger can turn any situation into an absolute nightmare. This is where the Stoic principles can prove to be of immeasurable value. The Discipline of Action, for example, can go a long way to helping a person to make decisions based on evidence rather than their emotional reaction. Even though you might still feel fear as a result of a situation, by controlling your decision making process you can be free from the domination that fear can bring. By using logic and wisdom you can make better choices, no matter what your emotions are telling you. This applies to anger as well. When you take control of your anger you prevent it from taking control of you. The Discipline of Action will ensure that you never react out of malice or rage, causing harm to friends or loved ones. Not only will this prevent the suffering that they would feel, but it also prevents the guilt and shame that you would experience after the fact.

The Discipline of Desire is another Stoic principle that goes a long way to freeing the mind. A person's emotions can cause them to crave and desire all sorts of things, regardless of what those things actually are. Even worse, when a person allows their desires to control them they run the risk of becoming addicted to things. Those things might be as seemingly innocuous as watching TV, shopping or using social media. Alternatively, those things might be more sinister, such as drugs, alcohol or gambling. At first, developing the Discipline of Desire can take a great deal of effort, especially if you suffer from addiction in any form. However, once you achieve the goal your mind will be free of the 'demons' of addiction, meaning that you are in control of your life once again. In this context the freedom from external and internal influences are very closely related. After all, advertising campaigns can't have an impact on your decision making process if there isn't an internal response to trigger. Therefore, by practicing the Stoic disciplines you will free your mind from all dangers, both those from without and those from within.

Freedom from Suffering

Finally there is the aspect of freedom from suffering. This might seem out of place when talking about how Stoicism frees the mind of the practitioner, however when you stop to consider the true nature of suffering it begins to make a whole lot of sense. If you look for alternate words for 'suffering' one that you will find is 'anguish.' And when you think of anguish you more often than not think of mental anguish, which takes place solely in the mind. Suffering, therefore, can be seen as a state of mind, meaning that you cannot free yourself from suffering unless you free your mind.

One way that Stoicism serves to free the mind of suffering is to put things into proper perspective. All too often what causes suffering in the first place is to desire things that are beyond reach, to fear things that are inevitable, or to try to control things that are beyond your control. The Discipline of Assent serves to put all of these things into context. By realizing that certain things are beyond your control you can let go of the responsibility of those things and their outcomes. Additionally, by accepting that some goals are beyond reach, and that certain things will happen whether you want them to or not, you can remove the frustration that those things bring. In the end, the key to eliminating suffering is to see things for how they really are. This frees the mind from trying to solve problems that it simply doesn't have the power to solve.

Another way to free the mind from suffering is to experience suffering willingly. This doesn't mean that you have to desire hardship, rather it means that you immerse yourself in hardship when it comes your way. The point of this exercise is to prove that you are stronger than the hard times you face. Proving that you can endure hardship will free your mind of the fear and dread that hardship engenders. Once you achieve this goal you will notice two consequences. First, you will find that hard times seem far less sinister and insurmountable than they once did. This liberates you from the emotional and mental distress that most experience during hard times. The second consequence is that when your mind is free of anguish it becomes more capable of solving the problems you face. Therefore, not only have you freed your mind of distress, but you have also freed-up your mind to better perform the tasks it was designed for in the first place, thereby bringing hard times to a quicker and happier end.

Understanding Emotions

Stoics always feel. This is not one of enthusiastic restraint. Despite what might be expected, it is an expectation of Stoics that quietness and euphoria are brought about by living your life to the fullest. All things considered, individuals appear to liken Stoics, to Vulcan wannabes. Nothing against Vulcans besides their paternalistic approach towards humankind in the pre-Federation years but there are bad stoic good examples like additional terrestrials. Stoics are understudies of being human.

The stoic maxim, live as indicated by nature, moves us to figure out where in this growing universe we fit in. Everything that is chaotic and totally bizarre in this world that connects life is included here. Doubtlessly, we concentrate the greater part of what is our consideration on human personality, which on its own is an astounding instrument. The mental scene is made up of feelings and this is where Stoics do give it their due. There is always that nagging thought of not fully commending them on their discovery.

In this passionate life, quite different from how we deal with it, Stoics have their own way of dealing with it. For example, we don't anticipate that feelings will be great aids for conduct. Climate can be a way to say how these feelings are treated like. You are required to drive slowly, carry an umbrella when there is rain, yet you need to work in the end. Passionate tempests are quite similar in a way. Despite having a terrible feeling towards some things, Stoics believe we can still act well at present.

If you're to a great degree inconsiderate to your associates and, when inquired as to why, you replied, "it's sticky," individuals would perceive you as amusing. Stoics would state that snapping at individuals since you're furious is similarly unreasonable. In the first place, your outrage itself is most likely because of receiving an unhelpful point of view. Second, regardless, a man has the option of acting with uprightness regardless of the situations.

There are three "positive sentiments" that Stoicism run by. In Greek, they are referred to as hai apatheia. These sentiments are Caution, Wish, and Joy. There are three Passions that are considered "awful sentiments" of Stoic reasoning. The distinction was created to separate the positive from the negative sentiments. In psyche, the Stoic lineup is...

Joy v. Pleasure

Wish v. Appetite (Lust)

Caution v. Fear

I wouldn't contend on the off chance that to you the rundown does look rather odd. It requires a background knowledge on this subject to see how people of old reached these conclusions, and, after it's all said and done, you may think they're nuts. Look at this article on Stoic morals on the off chance that you need a taste. As far as it matters for me, I need to bring up that Joy, Pleasure, and so forth are all-encompassing classifications.

Every one of the subtleties of human feeling can be categorized with one of these words, so don't stress over begrudge, covetousness, seethe, vindictiveness, etc..., they're altogether represented. Gracious and the fourth energy, Distress. Pain cannot be an inverse and Misery is troubling.

Next is Wish. It is a peculiar name for an enthusiastic idea. Why you might wonder, do Stoics consider Appetite awful and Wish great? It might be due to the fact that, according to the Marcus Aurelius citation I began with, take into consideration that this movement is entirely feasible for you to do. Stoics pin for things that you don't require or see as the tremendous misuse of vitality.

The definition of the energy Appetite according to us is, "the silly yearning or quest for a normal descent." Greed is a hunger for tangible/material things; whereas Hostility is the quest for vindicating. Our vitality is consumed by these things on a dream, or as they tend to do, make us perform useless activities. Things that are out of control are things that Stoics do not wager their joy on. They'd rather wish than accept Appetite.

According to Aurelius, you have to delight in your activity. When Stoics discuss feeling, it is always to influence; the cognizant, subjective part of a feeling that is considered separate from the real changes.

Hunger isn't about seeing a man who is per your standards, it is that inclination in addition to the prospect that keeps running with it, says

"Dammann NN," and afterward lines it all with a mental symbolism. The mental segment, according to Stoicism, is a decision, one that is undesirable. There can be a superior effect that can be asserted; Wish that is fulfilling and enduring too.

When you delight in an activity, it is always possible for you to get through it.

Wish is not known, but its influence states that it says "I should have x. However my satisfaction is not situated in x." in context, it is a move. The things that are to make you happy are Hunger. Wish on the other hand says that there are other fabulous things in the world, but I will not find my happiness in them. The first standard of Stoic is that having a wish like behavior is the main thing that is under our control and righteousness is the main great. It is conceivable to be content; this is according to Stoics point of view. It is not an easy feat, as there is no guarantee that going along with this is simple. Instead of Appetite, Wish is an influence that provides a true and rich ground to have insightful activities.

A comparative rationale is that of Caution versus Pleasure versus Fear. Fear is neglecting a normal threat and it makes us throw away the satisfaction we have at present because we think that something or someone will come and take it away from us. Caution is more of knowing that curveballs are going to be coming our way and it is up to us to be arranged at the same time, by and by, genuine peace isn't found in outer things. On the off chance that we will prosper, we should approach the world not with caution but with mindfulness.

Pleasure, according to the negative perspective of Stoics, is additional because of Joy's outer core interest. Stoic's try to build up a withstanding Joy, setup of momentary snapshots of pleasure. By and by, I don't attempt to debilitate the feelings of excitement that I have. I attempt to remember what makes me feel excited by need, be transient and it is quite conceivable to exist without such things.

As we said before, Stoics feel. "Walking it off" is not a rationale that we conclude on. We require and insist on the best for individuals, this is because of the standard low points and high points in our lives. We think that most of the agony we go through is self-delivered, this is as a result of a perspective that requires we see the world not as it is or in a similar way. Fragile, mortal things, expectation-past expectations- are the interests that we concentrate on the most such that they keep on. What is distinctive is Caution, Happiness, and Wish. This comes from a mind that acknowledges changes do happen; meaning that what is in us can thrive and survive.

Chapter 8

Deception

T he act of lying is a common phenomenon in the world. There are several reasons why people chose to be deceptive in their day-to-day lives. The act of deception can be done either for personal gain or for ideological reasons. The act is very dangerous because it has the potential to harm a victim. The process is always carried for a varied period of time that is considered by the person performing it. In fact, the act of deception is broad because it can be done without necessarily harming the victim being lied to.

There are several ways an individual can choose to understand what deception is. The best way to begin the process of deep understanding commences with knowing the definition of the term. The act of deception can be described as a process of making a person believe something that is not true. It entails a broad form of making a false reality through the manipulation of appearances. The current world has seen and experienced several forms of deceptions in several contexts. Therefore, it becomes a difficult task to categorize these forms of deception using a common feature in them. This is despite every act of deception, having a familiar resemblance to the others.

Deception contains both forms of simulation and dissimulation. Simulation is the act of withholding or hiding important information from the victim of the deceitful act. On the other hand, dissimulation is the process of putting out misleading or wrong information to an individual being deceived. Both the act of lying can be successful by either commission or omission of information. However, the moral compass times seem to support deception that is achieved by omission rather than that of commission.

The first group of a psychologist who studied the art of deception did their research in the year 1989. They did their study by looking at sleight of hand magic or conjuring as their paradigm. Conjuring can be described as one the acts in the world that an individual's ability to deceive is its success determinate. However, this form of deception has a major difference from that that is made by a confident person or a spy agent. It is because it has an element of a sanctioned form of deception. The person performing conjuring has a contract with his or her audience to fool the people watching him or her. Therefore, an individual would not be described as a good magician in events he or she fails to fool the audience. Also, the parties experiencing conjuring are always aware they are about to be fooled prior to the action.

However, the act of deception has a different way its success comes about. During the act of deception, the victims are not told or made aware of what is taking place or what is about to happen. There are several magic tricks that have been accepted by the current world. On the other hand, there are close to no forms of deceptions that have been sanctioned by the global society. It is because several communities across the globe have their moral compass conflicting with the act of lying. This is despite some forms of lying being tolerated and being sanctions in some groups of people. These forms of sanctioned lies include fantasies, fables, and jokes since they have little harm to society.

There are numerous depictions of deception and the context they have been used across the globe. There are moments of certain moments that teens or adolescents have been able to fool adults. The case does not occur only on teens or adolescents; there are several cases that varied people of ages and sex have been able to lie to doctors or other health practitioners. They would aim to avoid or change the prescriptions that they are given. Consumer Fraud in the health industry has been among the common case that has been highlighted in the current world.

The other form of deception that has been highlighted for a long time is known as military and strategic deception. This form of deception has been practiced since time immemorial by several communities or nations across the globe. Ploy and feints are very important and highly valued in sports and games as forms of deception. People such as gambling cheats, impersonators, and fraudulent psychics have increased in numbers across the world. This has made swindles and games of confidence taking a common fall on victims who are willing.

The criminal case of deception is commonly known as a forgery in various countries in the global village. Several people have drawn they're interested in knowing and understanding deception. This has seen publications such as books and journals focusing on plagiarism and other deception forms that are the scientific field. The other form of deception that has seen the rise of interests from sociobiology's, psychologists, and philosophers is known as self-deception.

These forms of deceptions are worth being looked at. However, the major focus is being put at face to face deception that entails two people communicating. This has led to several types of research in the psychology of a human being. Several people have been curious to know how to deceive other people or how to know the moments they are being deceived with other people. Such forms of deceptions are prone to occur when there is an actual exchange of information between people. It is determined by factors such as psychological issues and structural matters.

Theories, Taxonomies, and Frameworks

Several scientists tried to develop the psychology of deception in the late 19th century. They aided their research with the paradigm of conjuring as the case for deception. The aim of this research was to be able to classify the general principles that are used in conjuring while mystifying the audience. This will then form a base to explain the framework the act of deception works on. However, conjuring could not for the best paradigm because they are different acts, as noted above.

Therefore, this has led to the development of taxonomies to work as the framework for the theory of deception. A good taxonomy helps to contribute to the development of a theory that is adequate. This is made possible because taxonomy helps in directing the focus of an individual into a specific study. The first step of conducting taxonomy involves considering the process as extremely tentative. There are certain challenging circumstances that can be experienced during the process of the research survey. These challenges include; there are some categories that will lack representatives, and there will be other forms of study that will have difficulties fitting in these categories. However, a good taxonomy exercise is judged by its ability to help its users.

Several taxonomies on deception have been developed by several theorists. These taxonomies have a critical advantage to the current and next generation. It is because they will be used as a source of developing comprehensive deception systems in the current and the next generation. These systems can be pivotal in helping future investigations on deceptions. However, the most important aim of taxonomies is helping to develop scientific theories of deception.

Such a theory will have several components in it. It will comprise of basic variables, common concepts, and laws that will enable an individual to understand deception. The successful forms of taxonomies have been able to start with the actual definition of what deception is. It goes deeper to more scientific explanations of the phenomenon. These analyses take the common cases that occur in the daily life of human beings to be able to relate with people understanding of the concept.

Taxonomy in Psychological Space

During this taxonomy, a systematic relationship between the terms of deceptions and English speakers was studied. This study entails how forty-six terms were being related to deception. There were several theories that were invoked theories of deception that were acknowledged. Deception is able to encompass categories such as lies, masks, crimes, fiction, and playing. The forms of deceptions that have been practiced across the world tend to have a clear line of similarities among them. This form of taxonomy is very hierarchal. It is because the six categories can be grouped under two major categories.

The two major categories that characterize the six categories of deception are known as exploitative fabrications and benign fabrications. There are several things that are encompassed in benign fabrications which include playing and fiction. On the other hand, exploitative fabrications involve several activities such as underlies, masks, crimes, and lies. This taxonomy was a spearhead of two individuals during the 1980s. They were Mr. Hopper and Mr. Bell who went further to try looking into the forms of deceptions that morally acceptable, harmless and socially acceptable; morally unacceptable, harmful and socially unacceptable as new categories of deception taxonomy.

The first dimension was labeled as harmfulness. This dimension entails forms of deception that ranged from immoral, bad, harmful, and unacceptable. The terms used in dimension were termed as low rating words. High-rated terms were used to describe harmless, moral, and acceptable. The second dimension was labeled as covertness. The items on this dimension were rated highly were based on convert, nonverbal, and indirect—those who were rated lowly were based on verbal, direct, and covert.

Deception Tactics

The current world has seen several forms of deceptions that have been done. These activities have been done at home, work, and several social places. The common view from the wide global society puts this act as immoral.

Following an Unreasonable Request by a More Reasonable One

This tactic is used by several people who deceive others to get what they want. It can be described as a time-tested tactic of deception. If an individual does want to perform the act of deception, he or she is likely to make an unreasonable request as the first step. The unreasonable always has a high chance of being rejected. It is then followed by the second request, which tends to sound appealing to the target if compared to the earlier demand. This form of tactics has been used several times in the cooperate world. The best depiction can be seen when there is an involvement of actual buying and selling of goods or services.

Making an Unusual Request Prior to Making the Actual Request

The other way to make an individual do a task for you is by making unusual forms of requests. These kinds of requests have the ability to make an individual be swept away by being off guard while the request is being made. During these moments, it is always difficult for an individual to reject the request being made. However, going direct to the request and the individual's needs has high possibilities of an individual facing rejection right away. A good depiction can be used in a street if one needs to tie his or her shoe; he or she can first go-ahead to telling the target of a sprained back then go to the favor.

Instilling Fear and Relief

The process of deception entails an individual getting what he or she wants. This can be achieved when the target is firstly made to fear the worst. The second step in this technique involves making the person be relieved by sitting better possibilities. This makes an individual be happy and be in an able position to grant the person deceiving him or her to getting he or she wants. What this technique does entail is a little bit of trick and getting the end result desired.

Making the Deceived Party Feel Guilty

Guilt is a very deep form of emotion that is very critical in people's daily life. It is one of the most used tactics when people are supposed to get manipulated to doing certain things. The first step to this technique involves the picking of the right target to perform this technique. Most people who are preferentially picked are those who have the tendency to feel guilty most of the time. The second step is about ensuring the target picked is guilty about what the deceiving party wants. These parties can be business parties who have denied an individual a deal; it can be a parent or a friend also. The best way a friend is meant to be deceived is by being reminded of favors made to them by the deceiving party.

Usage of Bribery

Bribery is a common occurrence that is being witnessed across the world. It is described as one of the best ways an individual carrying out deceit can be able to achieve his or her act of manipulation. Bribery can be described as an act of offering another party something valuable in exchange with a form of favor. Valuables, in this case, can be money or other forms of offers. During the act of bribery, an individual conducting the act of deceit does not have to black his or her target.

The process is handled with finesse for it to be successful. The first step in this technique involves an individual researching on the most important values his or her party is in deer need of. People tend to be very desperate when they need certain things urgently, and they are way out of their reach. The second step involves the party practicing the manipulative act, not making his or her action seem obvious. They have a tendency to make their actions seem like a form of assisting the other party so as to hide their clear intentions.

Playing the Victim

Playing the victim during the act of deceit has the potential of making the act become successful. The process has its advantage, though—during deception, it is not supposed to be overdone. This makes the tactic to be used during certain moments and sparingly. The tactic is supposed to be able to hit the heart of the targeted victim. The manipulators tend to act in a way that they are altruistic and wonderful people. This is then followed by a deceiving act that several things in their world are crumbling. They tend to play dumb during the process and act pathetically.

Using of Logic

This technique has a certain group of people who it used on by manipulators. The category includes those people who are predicted to have a rational type of mind. These kinds of people tend to be easily persuaded with logical thinking. Therefore, manipulators tend to have at least three reasons to try convincing the target of deceit. These reasons tend to have advantages for both the manipulator and the target of deceit. These thoughts are always presented in a rational form so as to help the manipulator not to lose his or her cool. During these presentations, emotions tend to be drawn away for the manipulator to be able to reach his or her target mind.

Not Breaking of Character

This is a trick that nearly every successful manipulator practice. There are certain moments that a manipulator can be suspected by people or a person around him or her. During such moments, a person conducting his or her deceiving act cannot accept or admit to his or her actions. They are prone to turning the situation to the other party that had discovered them. It is because the process of deceiving a person the second time is hard if they had learned of one's actions earlier on.

Chapter 9

Neuro-linguistic Programming in Everyday Life

H ave you ever realized how powerful our mind is? You can think anything endlessly. The sky is literally the limit. You can envision yourself to be the person you want to be and make it into a reality. Every thought we have in our mind can trigger us to do something that is worth pursuing. That is how our conscious and unconscious mind works. If we want to achieve greater things in life, we focus on it and believe that we will attain it. It all boils down to how we think and deal with life opportunities and challenges.

We have discussed that NLP is a modeling approach that actually deals with how our mind can change the way we think, view past events, and approach our lives. This method molds the perception of people to think eloquently and analyze strategies towards the accomplishment of their personal goals. The neurons in our brain are all interconnected. We form our unique internal mental maps of the world as an outcome of the way we riddle and perceive data we captivated through our five senses. We then ascribe personal meaning to this information we receive from the world. By assigning a distinct language to these internal images, sounds, feelings, tastes, and smells, we form our second mental map. Thus, forming our conscious awareness. From the inner voices we hear in our minds, to the way we communicate through it, NLP is the core process to translate our insights into productive and worthwhile. There are many ways on how we can apply Neuro-Linguistic Programming in our everyday life. As a student, a parent, a worker, or an aspiring artist, we can always use NLP as our core process to aid our mind to be unstoppable in reaching our goals.

In this century, everything revolves around automation and instant gratification. Phones have become wireless, cooking became wireless, cars do not need keys nor gas to run. However, there is an irony to these improvements. The youth today are jobless and irresponsible. Relationships are meaningless and are defined by wealth and fame. Leaders have no sense of shame, especially in corruption. People become careless, envious, heartless, and cold. Education has become valueless because it is defined by grades not by learning. Lastly, children have become globally mannerless. People have houses, but not necessarily a comfortable home. We all have big and comfortable beds, but we cannot get enough sleep. There are a lot of new recipes to try, but people no longer have time for eating. Everything is just stressful – full of pressure, anxiety, and frustration.

Luckily, the hope to change these things is endless and ever burning. To some, people believe that this is their fate, their destiny. And nobody can change that. But through NLP, you will realize that we are the masters of our own fate. We are the captain of our own ship. We create our destiny.

Nobody makes our decisions but us. You control your environment. Your society does not control you. The reason why people these days are unhappy is the lack of contentment in their life. They like to conform to the norms of society. In turn, they become living robots without any sense of reality. To them, society is their reality. They do not realize that happiness is a state of mind. Wherever you are, whatever you do, if you put your heart into it, you will be happy.

In this segment, we will discuss how to reprogram your brain to finally have the happy and joyful life you deserve. See, there are three factors that program the brain – Environment, Education, and Experience. But these can be reprogrammed through Reframing, Renaming, and Retraining.

The reason why we remain pessimistic is the fear of reframing and retraining our mind to think about things differently. Because of our bad experiences, we are always scared to try again. We failed to see the positive thing during our first encounter, which is why we are hesitant to try again. But when you finally acquire the boldness to reframe your thoughts about a situation, you start to be stronger to face this challenge, and you can finally retrain your thought from a negative impression to a positive one. There are many steps to foster positivity and happiness in life. Neuro-Linguistic Programming recommends you do these following methods to foster a positive mindset on the way to a successful and happy life.

Strengthen your Relationships Every day. Whether it is to your friends our family members, it is very important to maintain a healthy relationship. Look at this as your personal network where you can be comfortable to open up your feelings. These people whom you trust are responsible for uplifting your spirit, guiding your thoughts and behaviors, and makes you feel positive no matter how difficult life is for you. These series of networks assure you that even if you fail, they always have your back. They will always be there especially when you need them the most. The love, care, and support you give to each other are priceless; it may serve as an inspiration for you to achieve your goals in the future. So, never let yourself take them for granted. Utilize the power of your gadgets and the internet. Even if you do not see them every day, make sure to give simple sentiments of care. These simple gestures can bring you and your loved one's joy and satisfaction. It makes you feel that you are not alone. So, you can sleep at night knowing people root for you.

Try new Things. Whether it is a change in career or experiencing new hobbies, trying new things can give you several insights and experiences you can use towards your development. Through Neuro-Linguistic Programming, you can be bold, strong, and courageous in going out of your comfort zone, taking on new challenges, and learning new things. Do not limit yourself to the schema you have developed in the past. No matter how old you are, there will always be new things to learn, beautiful places to see, and activities to experience. It is never too late to try anything that your heart desires. Because this is where you can find happiness, joy, contentment, and satisfaction in life.

Always Aim for Self-Improvement. This is one of the most important ways to break the chains that society has given you since birth. As we have discussed before, even if you think you have reached your full potential, there is still so much you need to know about yourself. Your current funds are limited because you let it fall in line with the standards of society. That you need to change that through Neuro-Linguistic Programming. In everything you do, aim for your own growth and development. Avoid remaining stagnant and idle, especially on the road to success. If you really want to reach your innermost desires, you need to learn how to get out of your comfort zone and start looking for opportunities where you can learn. Take advantage of your education and training. These could help you unlock a whole new level of potential. When it comes, do not be afraid to grasp it.

Foster Self-Discipline. Neuro-Linguistic Programming allows you to apply self-discipline every day in your life. When you have self-discipline, you start to control your mind little by little; piece by piece. Self-discipline is the key to achieving your goals. It helps you ward off any temptation that can derail you from your dreams. If you really want to lose weight, you need the self-discipline to say no to fatty foods and junk foods. If you want to quit smoking and drinking, maintain a sufficient amount of self-discipline to avoid being tempted into the black hole again. This also works when you want to avoid procrastination. Self-discipline allows you to control your mind and tell it to stay productive.

Learn to Assert Yourself. One of the main reasons why a person experiences depression and frustration is his lack of assertiveness. When a person lacks this skill, others are inclined to take him for granted. To people, it is okay for him to be picked last, to be bullied, and to be hurt. Because of these experiences, a person emulates helplessness. He starts to believe that he deserves his fate. Why let yourself be taken for granted when you can assert yourself? Learn to disagree from time to time. Share your opinions to people. Think of yourself and your feelings too. Do not let other people push you around like you are expendable. Remember that you are a human being; you have the right to live a happy and free life. Self-compassion is not a form of selfishness. In fact, it is a form of self-love. To achieve a satisfying life, do not let others take those rights away from you. Claim it for yourself not because you can but because you deserve it.

Pursue what you want. The common mistakes among people are that they live their life according to what their parents and society have dictated. In order to be truly happy, you need to learn how to say no to these standards and create your own. What do you really want to achieve in life? What to do you want to make? Do not rely on your parents to make these decisions for you; do it for yourself. Remember, you make your own fate and nobody else. You only live once to waste it by impressing people by doing what you do not want. Break those chains they have locked around your neck. The expectations and realities they have fed you is all an illusion. Create your own reality based on what you want it to be. Make it into something that fits your lifestyle, your talents, and your skills. As long as you are not stepping on other people's toes and your conscience is clear, you are free to pursue whatever you want whenever you want it.

When we desire to achieve great things in life, we always go back to reassessing ourselves and determining the approaches we need to take to get what we want. If you let yourself remain in a negative position, your emotions and actions are directly affected. Your mind could star to command impulses that you no longer have control of. This could take a toll on your social, emotional, psychological, and physical aspects.

If our mind is reprogramed to think optimistically, it is clear evidence that we will be able to do greater things ahead of us. It is a matter of believing in ourselves and overcoming the challenges we encounter. Like what Marcus Aurelius said, "The happiness of your life depends upon the quality of your thoughts." Therefore, we have to reprogram our thoughts in an optimistic way to get the satisfaction and contentment we always want.

Goal Setting Through NLP

Everyone talks about setting goals for a brighter future. May it be short or long-term. However, the journey to realizing our goals may not be something so easy to achieve. During the process, we sometimes overlook things and ended up on a bad side. For some, it may be difficult to recover while others are struggling to overcome the current crisis they are facing. But how does one set a goal and realize it despite the many trials he or she may encounter?

Goals are one of the greatest motivators in life which help us to comprehend our current state and focus on pursuing what our mind and heart desire. Very few of us are living the life we want. While some were born with a golden spoon, and others were not, there is no exemption as to who can dream about anything. However, there is something else that would be nice to have or do. That feeling of aiming and wanting to acquire something greater. We seem to program our mind to seek for more. We tend to often convince ourselves that we can only be happy unless we get it.

You might be wondering why New Year goals, of course, most of us tend to look forward to the new beginnings and change the bad habits in the previous year. With a new year ahead, goals are being set. Sadly, the reality is only eight percent of goal-setters do consistently and exceptionally well. They are said to be the successful ones in life.

In NLP, the acrostic S.M.A.R.T will help you define what you really want. This acronym stands for Specific, Measurable, Achievable, Realistic, and Timely. NLP introduces the concept of using a 'well-formed' outcome process – a process that makes your SMART goals even smarter. The S.M.A.R.T system has been proven to help individuals achieve their goals. It is, in fact, strong evidence on how we approach life challenges and how focus can we get to meet the ends. Neuro-Linguistic Programming, however, will give this a boost by adding sensory-specific information which helps to transform your behavior into such goal setter.

To overcome problems and reach out for excellence, the NLP helps us change the way we think, behave and communicate with ourselves and with others. This allows us to create and recreate our life the way we want it. This also provides a rapport of how people think and act to enable to influence others. To see how willing you are to dwell on setting goals and wanting to achieve them, you will need to answer a series of questions which will allow you to understand more about your reason. Say your desired outcome wants to land on a high paying job, you can ask questions like is the goal stated in positive? Is it self-initiated and within your control? Does the goal describe the evidence of the procedure? Is your goal not impossible to achieve? Does the goal identify the first step you need to take? These are just some of the questions which might enlighten you.

You must know what your desired result is because your focus must be into that direction for you to achieve it. You have to specify what you really want such as "I want to lose 30 lbs." which is clearer and more specific than saying "I want to lose weight." This approach is made up by "S" in the S.M.A.R.T system which means SPECIFIC. Do not set a goal too general because it might cause some drawbacks. To set a specific goal, your questions must be in W form like Who, What, Where, When, Which and Why. Getting more specific and goals in the positive form will help you to be more driven. If this is the case, your mind is programmed to wanting you to get fat rather than losing weight. Therefore, it is important to have set in mind in a positive manner statement.

The next approach of the goal setting is answering if is it self-initiated and within your control? This defines the M in S.M.A.R.T which is MEASURABLE. If your aim is to achieve a greater outcome, then it has to come for you. Your set goals must be realistic and not beyond your control. For example, if you want to have a high salary instantly, your choice will be seeking agent jobs in the BPO industry. On the other hand, you also want to work with your engineering course, but the salary is not in your expectation. As you see, you are confused about whether to follow what your heart desires or only think about practicality. The goal of having a high salary is in your hand and in your control. Thinking about "I want a high salary" is not a bad goal, but a better one might be more specific. How high can your salary get? How to get your expected salary by still working with your passion? These are some of the questions you need to identify to see if your goal is measurable.

The next to put in mind is if the goal is ACHIEVABLE. First and foremost, you identify goals that are more significant to you. Next, you seek methods on how to make it come true. Then develop the abilities, skills, attitude and financial capacity to achieve them. A goal is achievable once you clearly plot the steps on how to realize it and what are the methods you will do to make it happen.

Another to consider setting a goal is being REALISTIC. In order to realize your goal, you need to set in an objective manner which you are willing and able to work. It is your choice about how high your goal should be. You just have to make sure that setting it represents substantial progress. Setting higher goals will most likely easier to reach because there is a strong motivational force that drives you to do the things that will help you achieve your goal. Comparing to the low goals, you just do not exert much effort to it because you feel like not worth to exert effort. When you set high goals, just make sure it is something you can accomplish and believe that you are willing to work for it.

The last of S.M.A.R.T approach is TIME-BOUNDED. Setting a goal must have a certain time frame. If there is none, no sense of urgency will trigger you when to work on your set goal. If you want to lose 30 lbs., then when do you plan to lose it by? Answering it by "someday" is not going to help you out. However, with a certain time frame, you follow such as saying within 3 months, you have set your unconscious mind into motion to start working on your goal and be able to achieve it in a timely manner.

With Neuro-Linguistic Programming combined with S.M.A.R.T goal setting, you can program your mind to have an unstoppable focus on attaining your goals. Although during the processing period, it might not be easy due to unforeseen circumstances that may come your way. If you feel like starting to build up negative emotions because of your plans not able to be followed, do not veer off from what you have set. Instead, let your mind be programmed that trials are there to challenge you and you are a fighter to face them with courage. Realizing your goals is not just some easy-peasy thing to do because it is always about mind over matter. The willingness to pursue achieving your goals matters most. It always depends on you on how you will deal with it. Just make sure that during the process in attaining your goals, you do it with determination and passion, not for compliance sake. Your fruit of labor is much more appreciated if there is a will coming from you. Your own effort will be paid off when the right time comes, and once you achieve your desired goals, you then feel satisfaction and happiness about yourself and the things you have in life.

Conclusion

Neuro-linguistic programming promises happiness that transcends all those specifics. When you learn how to communicate, you can literally rule the world. There's no evil laughter in the background, though; it's a completely different kind of "ruling of the world."

It's the kind that allows you to rule, first and foremost, over your own kingdom of thoughts. It allows you to take control over who you are and who you project yourself to be out in the world. It allows you to be more in tune with yourself and more in tune with everyone else around you.

Over the course of history, words have taken over worlds more than once. Sadly, most of the time, it was the evil-doers that had the best words. We won't get into a political debate here, nor do we want to bum you out. But, for a brief second in time and space, imagine all the power of the 20th-century rulers unleashed toward the betterment of mankind.

And imagine that you can be part of the machinery that sets that in action. You can actually be the change you want to see in the world. You can actually be a person who understands people, who can empathize with them, who can manipulate them not in the negative sense, but in the sense of helping them find their own path.

That is what neuro-linguistic programming is all about. Perhaps not a coincidence, NLP was born in the wake of the post-WWII world, a world that had been torn apart by men who knew the power of words and what they can do when masses are wielded in one direction or another.

The way you use your language matters, precisely because language is the very essence of what you are as a human being. Unlike computers, you don't see zeros and ones. You always think in **words**. Every image you have in your head has a very tightly correlated set of sounds or, in some cases, a set of linguistic symbols you associate with it. That is how we are wired, and when you learn how to truly wire and unwire the patterns your brain has created all on its own, you can take control.

You can take control of your life. Of your own self. Of your negative emotions. Of every single small action that you may have been doing unconsciously. Of everything you want to achieve in your life.

We don't want to promise you the moon and then not deliver. We want you to experience the altitude of change NLP can bring into your life **on your own skin**. Hopefully, this book has given you the tools to create the NLP mind map you want in your life and the tools to help you create bridges of communication that will eventually get you every single thing you want.

NLP lingers at the border between science and art. It plays with language, but it taps into deeply scientific prerequisites. It uses strategy, but it calls for action that comes from the heart before anything. It paints the world map of your own brain, but it does so using data-driven color picking.

Take it, embrace it, work it into your life, and create the future you deserve. There's so much waiting for you beyond the horizon; you just have to dare to reach out and create the bridge that will take you there!